the
Formative
five

ASCD MEMBER BOOK

Many ASCD members received this book as a
member benefit upon its initial release.

Learn more at: **www.ascd.org/memberbooks**

Thomas R. Hoerr

the Formative five

Fostering Grit, Empathy, and Other **SUCCESS SKILLS** Every Student Needs

ASCD Alexandria, Virginia USA

1703 N. Beauregard St. • Alexandria, VA 22311-1714 USA
Phone: 800-933-2723 or 703-578-9600 • Fax: 703-575-5400
Website: www.ascd.org • E-mail: member@ascd.org
Author guidelines: www.ascd.org/write

Deborah S. Delisle, *Executive Director*; Robert D. Clouse, *Managing Director, Digital Content & Publications*; Stefani Roth, *Publisher*; Genny Ostertag, *Director, Content Acquisitions*; Julie Houtz, *Director, Book Editing & Production*; Liz Wegner, *Editor*; Georgia Park, *Senior Graphic Designer*; Mike Kalyan, *Director, Production Services*; Cynthia Stock, *Typesetter*; Andrea Hoffman, *Senior Production Specialist*

All web links in this book are correct as of the publication date below but may have become inactive or otherwise modified since that time. If you notice a deactivated or changed link, please e-mail books@ascd.org with the words "Link Update" in the subject line. In your message, please specify the web link, the book title, and the page number on which the link appears.

PAPERBACK ISBN: 978-1-4166-2269-7   ASCD product # 116043
PDF E-BOOK ISBN: 978-1-4166-2271-0; see Books in Print for other formats.

Quantity discounts: 10–49, 10%; 50+, 15%; 1,000+, special discounts (e-mail programteam@ascd.org or call 800-933-2723, ext. 5773, or 703-575-5773). For desk copies, go to www.ascd.org/deskcopy.

ASCD Member Book No. F17-2. ASCD Member Books mail to Premium (P), Select (S), and Institutional Plus (I+) members on this schedule: Jan, PSI+; Feb, P; Apr, PSI+; May, P; Jul, PSI+; Aug, P; Sep, PSI+; Nov, PSI+; Dec, P. For current details on membership, see www.ascd.org/membership.

Library of Congress Cataloging-in-Publication Data

Names: Hoerr, Thomas R., 1945– author.
Title: The formative five : fostering grit, empathy, and other success skills every student needs / Thomas R. Hoerr.
Description: Alexandria, Virginia : ASCD, [2017] | Includes bibliographical references and index.
Identifiers: LCCN 2016036550 (print) | LCCN 2016044406 (ebook) | ISBN 9781416622697 (pbk.) | ISBN 9781416622710 (PDF)
Subjects: LCSH: Moral education. | Affective education. | Life skills—Study and teaching. | Multiple intelligences—Study and teaching.
Classification: LCC LC268 .H58 2017 (print) | LCC LC268 (ebook) | DDC 370.11/4—dc23
LC record available at https://lccn.loc.gov/2016036550

26 25 24 23 22 21 20 19 18 17   1 2 3 4 5 6 7 8 9 10 11 12

the Formative five

Introduction

Character is higher than intellect.

—Ralph Waldo Emerson

About a decade ago, I attended a conference for principals that changed how I think about the purpose of schools and the focus of my work. One of the speakers, James Honan of the Harvard Graduate School of Education, asked us to consider the following question: "How do you know when your school is successful?" We thought silently to ourselves for a moment before engaging in animated discussions at our tables. After a few minutes, we shared our responses with Honan, who wrote them down on a paper attached to a large easel.

Unsurprisingly, answers included high test scores, strong graduation rates, good student attendance, and graduates being accepted at schools of their choice. Someone shouted out "winning sports teams," to which a wise person replied, "How about winning sports teams where everyone plays?" eliciting lots of smiles and affirming nods. Another person suggested that a good mark of success would be going a week without the toilets getting clogged and with no school bus delays. Again there were many smiles and nods. Others mentioned going a week with no discipline problems; still others, going a week with productively involved parents. A couple of folks, myself included, mentioned the value of students being engaged in learning. When we were all done sharing, Honan spoke.

"You're all missing the boat," he said.

The room was silent.

"These achievements are important," he continued, "but you should be asking yourselves whether your students are going to be productive and happy citizens at age 25, 45, and 65. What kinds of adults will they be? Will they be good spouses, good friends, and good parents? Will they be respectful and honest, and will they work to make the world a better place? Those are the qualities that we should be valuing and pursuing in our schools. And those are the measures of your school's effectiveness."

Our Challenges

Of course, Honan was right. We must teach students to read, write, and calculate, but that's only the beginning; those goals should form the floor, not the ceiling, of their education. Our timeline is too short and our aspirations are too low if we limit our curriculum and pedagogical focus to tests, grades, and diplomas. We must step back and look at what's needed to achieve success in the real world, not just in school.

Although it has not been a significant part of the dialogue among educators, the distinction between what is needed to succeed in school versus out of it is one that writers and leaders have talked about for some time. Among the implications of Tom Friedman's "flattened world" (2005), for example, is that our workers increasingly compete against people who live thousands of miles away in other countries, rendering traditional scholastic skills important but insufficient. As Friedman put it more recently, "Thanks to the merger of, and advances in, globalization and the information technology revolution, every boss now has cheaper, easier access to more above-average software, automation, robotics, cheap labor and cheap genius than ever before" (2012). We need to prepare our students to be adaptable and flexible to meet a future in which the only constant will be change.

Friedman is not alone in expressing concern; there is a growing awareness that our graduates will need much more than mastery of the three Rs to make it in the world. As Kay and Greenhill (2012) note, "Doing well in school no longer guarantees a lifelong job or career as it did for previous generations of Americans . . . only people who have the knowledge and skills to negotiate constant changes and reinvent themselves for new situations will succeed" (p. xvii). Paul Tough, referring to those who question the "cognitive hypothesis" of academic accomplishment being the singular key to success, says, "What matters most in a child's development, they say, is not how much information we can stuff into her brain in the first few years. What matters, instead, is whether we are able to help her develop a very different set of qualities, a list that includes persistence, self-control, curiosity, conscientiousness, grit, and self-confidence" (2012, p. xv).

Henry Cloud makes a similar point in his 2006 book *Integrity*. After describing the traditional skills that are commonly associated with leadership, he cites the greater importance of factors that are not generally considered part of schools' curriculum or measured on scholastic tests. The qualities that determine good leaders, says Cloud,

> have little to do with IQ, talent, brains, education, training, or most of the other important components of success. Instead, they have to do with the other aspects of character functioning that we pay way too little attention to in training people to be leaders and to be successful. *The most important tool is the person and his or her makeup, and yet it seems to get the least amount of attention and work.* Mostly, we focus on professional skills and knowledge instead. (p. 10)

Similarly, Jensen (2012) cites research by the Carnegie Institute of Technology showing "that 85 percent of your financial success is due to skills in 'human engineering,' your personality and ability to communicate, negotiate, and lead. Shockingly, only 15 percent is due to technical knowledge."

As difficult as it is to transition from the cognitive hypothesis to a focus on success in life after graduation, we really have no choice: continuing to teach the same content does a disservice to our students. We cannot be deterred by fear from venturing into the nonscholastic realm. To quote Lisa Firestone (2016):

> Too often, we tend to think of our kids as less sophisticated and incapable of processing or understanding the emotional complexities of their world. We think we're protecting them by not bringing up the trickier, less pleasant subjects. But I can tell you firsthand that kids absorb a tremendous amount. Pretty much as soon as they're verbal, children can be taught to identify and communicate their feelings. In a trusted environment where emotions are talked about openly, most kids will speak freely about their feelings and are quick to have empathy for their peers.

In *Social Emotional Learning: Opportunities for Massachusetts and Lessons for the Nation* (2016), Rennie Center and ASCD note that success "in our increasingly dynamic global society requires students to develop skills that extend far beyond mastery of academic content" (p. 1). They continue:

> Various terms have been used to refer to these abilities, such as noncognitive skills, soft skills, or 21st century skills. More important, however, is the growing acknowledgment that students' social and emotional learning (SEL)—or the processes through which students and adults acquire and effectively apply the knowledge, attitudes, and skills necessary to understand and manage emotions, set and achieve positive goals, feel and show empathy for others, establish and maintain positive relationships, and make responsible decisions is critical to developing competencies besides academic content knowledge that are necessary to succeed in college and in careers. (p. 1)

Perhaps the need for this book is captured best by Smith, McGovern, Larson, Hillaker, and Peck (2016):

Not long ago, success in school meant success in life. We also believed that things like grit and determination were traits people were born with, not skills that could be developed over time. Over the past few decades, hard and soft sciences have produced an impressive body of evidence that teaches us two very new, very important things. First, that we can take our innate abilities and cultivate them, just like we build up muscle, dexterity, and language fluency. And secondly, that social and emotional skills matter just as much in determining life satisfaction and success as traditional intelligence. The use of the word "skills" here is intentional. These qualities are not only innate. They can be taught. And, they can be learned. (p. v)

Our Solution

Who you are is more important than what you know—to me, this phrase captures the priorities that we as educators must embrace. For years I've cited it at faculty meetings, during back-to-school nights, and I refer to it in my weekly letters to parents (see Appendix B). This isn't to denigrate scholastic knowledge or traditional learning in any way—absolutely, students do need to learn to read, write, and calculate. Rather, I repeat the phrase—*who you are is more important than what you know*—to make the sentiment an integral part of our school culture. And I believe that I've been successful: for example, the first page of students' New City School report cards is now devoted to sharing their progress on the personal intelligences (confidence, motivation, problem solving, responsibility, effort and work habits, appreciation for diversity, and teamwork). We also begin parent-teacher conferences by talking about students' strengths and weakness in these areas.

Of course, it hasn't always been easy. Investing time and energy in areas that may not lead to higher test scores or broadening the curriculum to include nonacademic spheres of instruction can be an uphill struggle. At our school, some teachers struggled to focus their instruction and assessment on less measurable areas because they were trained solely to measure success (both their students' and their own) according to progress in the three Rs. We spent time talking at faculty meetings not just about how we would determine students' progress in the personal intelligences, but about why it was important to do so. The messages our graduates sent helped: they would talk about how valuable it was for them to appreciate and work with peers of different races and socioeconomic levels. Sometimes teachers would focus one of their professional goals on how to teach "the personals."

Our faculty also read books—typically during the summer, but occasionally as part of a committee's work—that reinforced the message: *who you are is more important than what you know.* Daniel Goleman's *Emotional Intelligence* (1995) was one of them, as was Melba Beals's *Warriors Don't Cry* (1994). We read Beals's account of being one of the Little Rock Nine for what it had to reveal about our nation's racial consciousness and progress, but it was also a way to learn about and admire Beals's personal intelligences.

As with some of our teachers, some of our students' parents also found it hard to accept a wider definition of our goals and broader focus of our efforts. During large meetings with parents, I found that one effective technique of addressing this was to begin by asking parents to think of successful people they know—making a point not to provide a definition of *successful*. I would give them a minute or so to think and then ask them to talk in groups of three or four. After a few more minutes, I would ask the parents how many of them used income as a measure of success. A small number of hands went up. Then I would ask how many used qualities related to personal intelligences as criteria instead (e.g., working well with others; making a difference in the world; being good parents, spouses, and friends)—and a forest of hands would go up!

"The characteristics you are using," I would say, "are what we have listed on the first page of your students' report cards. We cannot stop with simply teaching students the three Rs."

The continued need to explain our rationale for measuring personal intelligence is not a surprise, because our schools have been focused almost exclusively on academic outcomes. Many parents naturally antic-ipate that the education their children receive in school will mirror their own experiences. The "cognitive hypothesis" to which Tough refers is strong!

The Purpose of This Book

I have high hopes for the difference that this book can make. It is designed to be an asset for teachers and principals to use in preparing their students for success beyond school—students who will be kind and caring people, responsible and productive workers, and citizens who make a positive difference in the world. Of course, such outcomes are the result of the incredibly hard work that parents and educators do to make a difference for young people. This book is meant to be a useful tool for them to use in that quest.

A Word on Terminology

Perhaps the most common phrase used to describe the important quali-ties that are not captured on standardized tests is *noncognitive skills*. I find the term *noncognitive* awkward; it is rooted in something that is *not* rather than in something that exists, which makes it hard to garner enthusiasm for it despite its ubiquity and the importance of what it represents. An example of the power of terminology comes from Howard Gardner, cre-ator of the theory of multiple intelligences. He has noted that his theory would not have generated so much enthusiasm if he had called it the theory of multiple talents.

So, what *should* we call the important qualities that are not assessed in standardized testing? *Social-emotional learning* is frequently used, as are *emotional intelligence* (Goleman, 1995) and *personal intelligences* (Gardner, 1983). From this point on, I will be referring to these areas of learning as *success skills*, because I believe that they will promote success in every arena of life.

The Formative Five Success Skills

It was no easy task to determine which skills to select for the Formative Five. After all, there's at least one for every letter in the alphabet:

- Acceptance
- Bravery
- Creativity
- Diplomacy
- Engagement
- Friendliness
- Generosity
- Helpfulness
- Insight
- Judiciousness
- Kindness
- Loving
- Magnanimity
- Nurturing
- Optimism
- Persistence
- Questioning
- Responsibility
- Sincerity
- Truthfulness
- Understanding
- Vigorousness
- Warmth
- Xenial
- Youthfulness
- Zest

Thank goodness there are only 26 letters in the alphabet!

Although each of the qualities listed above has merit, it is important that we focus our efforts on those factors that are the most significant. To that end, I've identified the following five formative skills necessary for success in both the work world and relationships of all kinds:

- Empathy
- Self-control
- Integrity
- Embracing diversity
- Grit

There also is another set of skills—courage, curiosity, responsibility, and receptivity—that is quite important to success in the real world, but I believe that all of these qualities inhere in the Formative Five:

- **Courage:** This is really a combination of integrity, self-control, and grit. Courage is having the integrity to know the correct path, as well as the self-control and grit to pursue it. Integrity requires courage, too.
- **Curiosity:** This is embedded in empathy and embracing diversity, both of which lead us to get to know and understand people from unfamiliar backgrounds.
- **Responsibility:** Very similar to self-control, this requires us to take ownership of our goals and have the grit to follow through.
- **Receptivity:** This skill is about being open to new ideas and experiences, which is at the root of empathy and embracing diversity. Understanding and appreciating others dissuades us from egocentrically believing that only existing practices and attitudes are worthy and that new ideas are to be shunned.

I recognize that identifying an absolute set of attributes is a bit like determining how many angels can dance on the head of a pin: it can't really be done. But I do believe that the Formative Five encompass the skills and understandings that we want our students to possess.

I realize that reasonable people can choose to focus on a different set of success skills, or on more or fewer attributes. My goal was to select ones that are important in every setting. Developing and cultivating these attributes in our students will greatly increase the likelihood that they will find success as adults, however they define it. In a sense, the Formative

Five are all "habits of mind" (Costa & Kallick, 2008)—that is, they reflect an individual's sense of self and his or her relationship to others.

Two of the Formative Five success skills—empathy and embracing diversity—are relationship-oriented; that is, they define how individuals orient themselves and behave toward others. In contrast, the other three skills—self-control, integrity, and grit—are self-oriented: focused on how we frame and control our thoughts and actions. Each of the Formative Five success skills reflects an aspect of Gardner's personal intelligences: empathy and embracing diversity are primarily interpersonal in nature, whereas self-control, integrity, and grit are intrapersonal. How Gardner's personal intelligences, Goleman's emotional intelligence, and the Formative Five interrelate is shown in Figure 1.

Of the five skills, only one—embracing diversity—requires a verb to connote its depth. That's because simply having a mix of demographics in the classroom isn't enough; educators must actively *embrace* the concept. Self-control, integrity, and embracing diversity are all discussed in Gardner's *Five Minds for the Future* (2006), and they are implicit in David Brooks's term "legacy virtues" (2015). Indeed, most leadership books refer to the Formative Five attributes even if the exact terms aren't the same (see Figure 2 for associated terms for each of the five skills). For

---

FIGURE 1

Emotional Intelligence, the Personal Intelligences, and the Formative Five

Focus	Goleman's Emotional Intelligence	Gardner's Personal Intelligences	The Formative Five
Self-oriented	• Self-awareness • Self-management	Intrapersonal intelligence	• Self-control • Integrity • Grit
Relationship-oriented	• Social awareness • Relationship management	Interpersonal intelligence	• Empathy • Embracing diversity

FIGURE 2	
The Formative Five Success Skills and Associated Terms	
The Formative Five Success Skills	**Associated Terms**
Empathy	Caring, understanding, compassionate
Self-control	Measured, restrained, disciplined
Integrity	Honest, trustworthy, respectful
Embracing Diversity	Tolerant, accepting, culturally responsive
Grit	Tenacious, resilient, fortitude

example, Stanley McChrystal discusses them in his book *Team of Teams* (2015), and Brené Brown's *Rising Strong* (2015) focuses on the need to cultivate empathy, self-control, and integrity. Perhaps not surprisingly, each of the Formative Five success skills can also be applied to Abraham Lincoln as depicted in Doris Kearns Goodwin's *Team of Rivals* (2005).

Significantly and encouragingly, *the Formative Five skills are teachable,* regardless of the students' ages. Of course, it is most effective to teach the skills when students are younger and more receptive, but they must be taught regardless of when this happens, because students can always learn to adopt them. By contrast, traditional measures of intelligence are fairly rigid and harder to improve upon. As Tough (2012) notes, "Pure IQ is stubbornly resistant to improvement after about age eight. But executive functions and the ability to handle stress and manage strong emotions can be improved, sometimes dramatically, well into adolescence and even adulthood" (p. 48). Empathy, self-control, integrity, and grit are all component parts of executive function.

How to teach the Formative Five is the focus of this book. By going beyond what is required to achieve standardized test success, educators can better prepare their students for life outside of school. Teachers can design their curriculum and teaching strategies to help students develop the Formative Five regardless of the type or level of school, and principals can create a larger context by addressing the physical setting—the halls and walls—and their expectations for staff, students, and parents to support such a focus. In a school committed to instilling the Formative Five in students, everyone works together to prepare students for the real world.

When I use the term *teaching*, I mean much more than simply formal instruction and dedicated lessons, although they are very important; rather, I mean *all* interactions among adults and students. Modeling skills, bringing students together to discuss issues, and framing the school's values—that is, what we say, do, and display—are all parts of "teaching." Nell Sears, the director of studies at the Friends School of Portland, Maine, puts it well: "Values are taught best when they are a core part of the school culture" (personal communication, February 1, 2016).

My Journey

Because our biases frame our thinking and determine how we envision schools, learning, and leadership, we must delve within to ascertain what we value before looking outside and taking action. Simply put, our perceptions form our reality; we act upon what we see. With that in mind, I'd like to share my educational background, perceptions, and principles of learning so that you can more fully understand where I'm coming from. I write as a former teacher and principal, but mostly as a student of learning—although I was not always receptive to it. My experiences are captured by what Winston Churchill once said: "I am always ready to learn, although I do not always like being taught."

For three years, I served as the principal of a high-poverty school in which standardized test scores were given much weight, so my suggestions in this book can be implemented in schools facing similar challenges. (Candidly, despite the 2015 passage of the Every Student Succeeds Act, I am not confident that we will be able to move away from overrelying on standardized tests as curriculum frameworks and measures of progress. I hope that I am wrong.)

For 34 years, I led a multiple intelligences (MI) school: New City School in St. Louis, Missouri. This MI experience widened my perspective and caused me to think in new ways not only about how we teach and assess but also about *what* we should teach. Although the faculty and I believed that all eight of the multiple intelligences are important, we felt that the personal intelligences should carry the most weight. This perspective—that focusing on mastering oneself and establishing relationships with others is critical to student success—frames my thinking.

For a decade, I have written the "Principal Connection" column in *Educational Leadership* magazine, contributed to education blogs, and written many articles and books. I agree with writer Joan Didion who said, "I write entirely to find out what I am thinking" (1980). Writing has caused me to reflect on both the goals of education and the ways that leaders can help children and adults grow.

For the past six years, I have led the Independent Schools Association of the Central States (ISACS) New Heads Network, a program that I helped create to support new school leaders at independent schools in the Midwest, and for three years I served on the ISACS's board of trustees. I am also currently a faculty member at the College of Education at the University of Missouri–St. Louis, working to prepare principals in the School Leadership for Innovation and Design Program. In each of these roles, I have been fortunate to participate in many discussions about how school leaders—both teachers and principals—can facilitate change that leads to good outcomes for students.

My Seven Principles of Learning

Here are the seven principles of learning that have guided me in writing this book:

1. **Constructivism:** We learn by creating and by making meaning. This is true for children as well as adults; in fact, we are all much more alike than different in how we learn. The best lessons are a combination of explanations and activities.

2. **Collegiality:** The quality of a school is determined by how well faculty members learn with and from one another (Barth, 1990). Teachers and principals embrace collegiality by serving as resources for one

another. The principal's job is to help everyone in the building grow and learn—starting with the faculty.

3. **Multiple intelligences:** We each have a different intelligence profile and we all learn differently. Opportunities to use a range of intelligences in our learning increase our capacity to learn and should therefore be routine. Using MI in teaching also allows students to learn by doing.

4. **Principal leadership:** The principal's job is not to make teachers or students happy. Happy teachers and happy students will certainly be more effective and productive, but happiness comes from growth. The principal's job is to create a setting where everyone grows by learning, and strong leaders create an environment where people are willing to step out of their comfort zones.

5. **Teacher leadership:** In good schools, leadership is not identified by a title. Though principals may be primarily responsible for many decisions, teachers also play vital leadership roles by implementing plans and working to help students succeed. This is particularly the case when the focus is on the Formative Five skills, which require teachers to use novel approaches with students, parents, and colleagues.

6. **Role models:** All adults in a school need to visibly "walk the talk." They must embody and display the success skills that they want to develop in students. In addition to helping students improve on their skills, educators should be comfortable sharing their journeys, both successes and failures, with students.

7. **Parental involvement:** Because students learn best when their parents are involved in their learning, teachers need to inform parents about their goals for their students and engage them in the work of meeting those goals. Teachers and principals need to prioritize parental involvement, devoting the time and energy necessary to help parents understand what is happening in their children's school.

I believe that these seven learning principles hold true for all schools, but particularly for those focused on the Formative Five skills, which are best learned through active engagement. Teachers will use role-plays, simulations, and experiential activities so that students can experience success skills in action. Settings where learners of all ages come to under-standing by doing, reflecting, getting out of their comfort zones and tak-ing risks, working collaboratively, reflecting again, and beginning anew are places where learners are bound to thrive.

The Importance of Transparency

The principles of learning on which the advice in this book rests are all predicated on transparency. Agendas are difficult to enact if they are not made public or if there exists confusion about the reasons for enacting them. Believe me, I've learned that even when I had the "right" solution (not often!), it wasn't *fully* right until others at the school embraced it. Maybe there was a time when top-down solutions worked well (although I doubt it), but if there was, it's certainly no longer the case. If we want our colleagues to be effective in pursing the Formative Five (or any other thrust, for that matter), they need to understand our thinking and be part of the solution. Leaders don't have a patent on knowledge, par-ticularly when it comes to sensitive and unconventional issues. Trans-parency at every level—with faculty, with students, and with students' parents—is absolutely essential. Leaders need to share their goals and plans for teaching the Formative Five with all stakeholders as often as possible: at the student assembly on the first day of school, at faculty committee meetings, in correspondences with parents, on the signs that hang on the walls, and so on. When asked to describe the school, every member of the school community should be able to easily discuss the importance of the Formative Five; educators should explicitly and rou-tinely use the term *success skills* so that it's on everybody's lips.

How We Got Here

Formal, large-scale schooling began in the United States well over a cen-tury ago with a focus on the 3 Rs. Much more recently, the focus has only gotten stronger since the release of the National Commission on

Excellence in Education's landmark 1983 report, *A Nation At Risk: The Imperative for Educational Reform*, which criticized the state of U.S. education and recommended "that schools, colleges, and universities adopt more rigorous and measurable standards, and higher expectations, for academic performance and student conduct, and that 4-year colleges and universities raise their requirements for admission" and that "significantly more time be devoted to teaching the New Basics." Of course, the vast majority of improvement efforts since the report's release have been tied to academic performance. Student conduct, though essential to student success, has received hardly any attention.

The federal government has continued to insert itself into educational policy and goals since 1983, most notably with the No Child Left Behind (NCLB) legislation of 2001 and the Department of Education's Race to the Top campaign, which began in 2009. These political thrusts into the educational arena vary in the details but share a laser-like focus on academics and standardized measures of student progress and school effectiveness. In some cases, data from standardized tests have been used to determine whether or not schools remained open or educators' contracts were renewed. Naturally, the result of these federal policies has led to a highly test-focused educational system. In many communities, schools' performances on standardized tests are featured on the front page of the local newspaper. In today's world of pervasive technology and instantaneous communication, it is quick and easy to embrace data that are reliable without questioning whether they are valid; we compare schools by using numbers regardless of whether or not they provide a full picture of what's being assessed.

On the official White House blog, U.S. Secretary of Education Arnie Duncan notes that "although well-intended, the No Child Left Behind Act . . . has long been broken. We can no longer afford that law's one-size-fits-all approach, uneven standards, and low expectations for our educational system" (2015). As assessment guru Grant Wiggins often put it, "what you measure is what you value," so it is no surprise that curriculum has been designed to drive standardized test results and that teachers and principals have worked diligently to improve students' performance on these tests (Hoerr, 2009). In *Harvard* magazine, David Perkins notes that "it's clear that NCLB has not worked well" and warns that the intense pressure it has caused can lead to cheating (Hough, 2015).

Every child attending a school under the NCLB's sword of Damocles has suffered to a degree because we have placed success on standardized tests ahead of developing the whole child. The focus on test metrics has narrowed curriculum and, in some schools, led to limiting the teaching of such subjects as art and music. In virtually all schools, devoting time to disciplines that are not directly tied to test scores has become less of a priority than ever.

Teachers and principals routinely complain about the amount of time they must spend preparing for and implementing standardized tests—a concern recently echoed by President Obama, who in 2015 "called for capping standardized testing at 2 percent of classroom time and said the government shares responsibility for turning tests into the be-all and end-all of American schools" (Associated Press, 2015). It was also noted that students take standardized tests for 20–25 hours per year and "between pre-K and 12th grade, students take about 112 standardized exams, according to the council report. It said testing amounts to 2.3 percent of classroom time for the average 8th-grader" (Associated Press, 2015).

Fortunately, the educational landscape appears to be tilting a bit. In December of 2015, President Obama signed the Every Student Succeeds Act (ESSA), "a sweeping rewrite of the No Child Left Behind act that returns power to states and local districts to determine how to improve troubled schools" (Davis, 2015). Though mandatory standardized tests for reading and math remain, state and local officials can now decide for themselves how to measure student progress and school success. The likelihood of schools being closed as a result of students' poor performance on standardized tests will now be greatly reduced.

As the passing of the ESSA indicates, people are starting to push back against the overemphasis on test results. Educators increasingly recognize that we must lead children to grow in ways that are not captured by standardized measures. A salient example of this sentiment is the ASCD Whole Child approach (www.ascd.org/wholechild), which reminds us that we must consider all aspects of children's growth, including safety and health.

1

Thinking About Tomorrow

Humanity will change more in the next 20 years than in all of human history.

—Thomas Frey

Like many of you, I've read lots of projections and scenarios about what the future might hold for education. So much is changing at such an amazing pace that it's hard to keep track of it all. This fact smacked me between the eyes when I read a *New York Times* article about dead people coming back to life:

Andy Kaufman and Redd Foxx to Tour, Years After Death, as Holograms

As comedians, Redd Foxx and Andy Kaufman could hardly be more different. Foxx, the pioneering nightclub performer and star of *Sanford and Son*, who died in 1991, was candid, socially conscious, and unapologetically obscene. Kaufman, the standup, sometime wrestler, and 'Taxi' costar, who died in 1984, was experimental, obtuse, playful, and perplexing.

But now these two comics will be united in a most unlikely way: Both are being turned into holograms to perform and tour again.

On Friday, Hologram USA, a technology company that spe-
cializes in these visual recreations of celebrities, announced that
it would use the likenesses of Kaufman and Foxx and parts of
their previously recorded routines to create hologram shows that
will be presented across the country next year. (Itzkoff, 2015)

No, I am not making this up. But as I think about it, I should not have
been that surprised. Ray Kurzweil predicted this blurring of reality and
illusion in his book *The Age of Spiritual Machines* (1999), envisioning a
future in which holograms appear so lifelike that the only way to determine whether the teacher at the front of the classroom is human is to
reach out and feel either flesh or air.

As it happens, holograms have been passing as living humans for
some time. The Lincoln Presidential Museum in Springfield, Illinois,
opened in 2005, features a presentation by an actor who, it turns out,
is really a hologram. I was there a few years ago, and the illusion was
so effective that it took me quite a while to realize that the figure I was
watching wasn't a human after all.

Consider, too, the Cisco Connected Classroom at the University of
Pennsylvania, as described by Ariel Schwartz (2013): "a floor-to-ceiling
screen at the front of each connected room for the lecturer, two smaller
80-inch screens on each side to display notes and guests beaming in
from elsewhere, and two mid-sized screens in the back to show students
in the other classroom." Although there aren't any holograms per se,
the life-size moving image of an instructor operating in real time and
beamed in from another continent challenges traditional conceptions
of classroom teaching. Returning to the idea of teacher holograms discussed at the beginning of this chapter, the future is closer than we think.
Here's the first line from an article on Ray Kurzweil's website about
robots possibly replacing teachers: "Researchers in the Personal Robots
Group at the MIT Media Lab, led by Cynthia Breazeal, PhD, have developed a powerful new 'socially assistive' robot called Tega that senses the
affective (emotional/feeling) state of a learner, and based on those cues,
creates a personalized motivational strategy" (Angelica, 2016).

Taking another step into the future, Ray Kurzweil posted an article to his website titled, "How to Animate a Digital Model of a Person from Images Collected from the Internet" (2015). What's next? Might we go to a theater to see John F. Kennedy debate Ronald Reagan? Surely we have libraries of videotape featuring the two presidents, so it's not at all a far-fetched possibility. And from there, how difficult would it be to bring portraits and pictures alive so that we can watch Abraham Lincoln discussing slavery with Christopher Columbus? If we can consider whether or not to use DNA extracted from fossils to bring dinosaurs that died 65 million years ago back to life, then creating holograms of long-deceased people using their DNA or that of their ancestors is not out of the question. Still, it all makes me very uncomfortable. Perhaps it would be a good topic to discuss during intermission at the Red Foxx and Andy Kaufman performance.

The Future, in General

Much of the rapid pace of change that we're experiencing is due to the invention of and rapid spread of new ways to communicate. Today, for better and or worse (actually, for better AND worse), we are almost always connected. For example, each day there are 100 billion e-mails sent and 300 billion Facebook posts made; last year, 200 billion tweets were sent. That's a lot of keystrokes! And according to *The Atlantic* magazine, 935,951,027 websites existed in September of 2015 (Lafrance, 2015). To put that in perspective, it would take 18 years to spend just one minute on each of those websites, excluding breaks for eating, sleeping, or walking the dog. My smartphone gives me access to the world's libraries and to millions of people. There is no doubt that the technology explosion has changed our lives for the better—but there is also no doubt that it has come at a cost.

A commentator on the *NBC Nightly News* recently noted that a study of low-income parents in Philadelphia showed that "nearly half of children less than a year old used a mobile device each day, and by the age of two, that percentage jumped up to nearly 80 percent." Dr.

Matilde Irigoyen of the Einstein Medical Center in Philadelphia added that "by age four, most (of the children) owned their own personal device" (2015). Parents and caregivers frequently use technology to keep young children occupied. And as everyone working in a school knows, it doesn't get any easier as kids get older.

Albert Einstein once said, "I never think of the future. It will come soon enough." Educators don't have that luxury. We must anticipate what the future will hold in order to prepare our students for tomorrow, but predictions are always uncertain. Here are two notorious examples (Lewis, 2013): In 1962, Decca Records passed on signing the Beatles to a contract, with one executive commenting, "We don't like your boys' sound. Groups are out. Four-piece groups with guitars, particularly, are finished." And in 2007, Microsoft CEO Steve Ballmer said, "There's no chance that the iPhone will get any significant market share. No chance." (See these and other equally bad predictions at www.buzzfeed.com /lukelewis/26-shockingly-bad-predictions.) Difficulty anticipating the future isn't limited to trying to determine what consumers will purchase. We have all seen the photo of President Harry Truman triumphantly displaying the newspaper proclaiming his loss to Governor Thomas Dewey in 1948, for example. More recently, the weekend before the national election in November 2012, Mitt Romney's campaign committee installed a $25,000 firework display in Boston Harbor in anticipation of Romney's election. According to a 2012 blog post by Eric Randall on the website of *Boston* magazine, Romney "and Paul Ryan seemed to truly believe the polls were 'skewed' to overestimate the numbers of minority and young voters that would show up to the election." For years I've been foolishly predicting that the St. Louis Rams—remember them?— would win more games than they would lose, and for years I've been proven wrong. (And don't get me started on those stocks that I was sure would increase in value!)

Perhaps Peter Drucker said it best: "Trying to predict the future is like trying to drive down a country road at night with no lights while looking out the back window." But our students' futures are too important for us not to at least try to anticipate what they will need and how we can best serve them. Driving down that metaphorical dim road, I see six trends that will inform how we need to prepare our students to achieve success in tomorrow's real world. Three of these trends are contextual—that is, they are worldwide thrusts that will have a strong effect on education. The other three trends are education-specific—they reflect ways in which schools will change. Each of these trends will result in the Formative Five success skills playing a prominent role in future school curriculums.

Contextual Prediction 1: The Earth Will Become More Fragile

Climate change will have a dramatic effect on how we live and work. Rising seas and more extreme weather will make it impossible to deny that it is happening, so conserving energy and protecting the planet will become immediate priorities. Unfortunately, much of the damage to Spaceship Earth has already been done, and it will take sustained effort by much of the world to halt it, let alone reverse it. The fragility of our ecosystem will result in much greater levels of environmental awareness and efforts by educators.

I do not anticipate the dystopia that James Kunstler predicts in his 2005 book, *The Long Emergency*, with skyscrapers abandoned because there's not enough power to operate the elevators. But there's no doubt that we will be forced to live differently—and, most likely, less comfortably. Potable water will become a scarce resource in many places, weather patterns will turn increasingly disruptive, and global disparities in wealth and comfort will grow larger and larger.

Writing for *National Geographic*, Tim Folger (2015) asserts that global warming projections from 2012 are actually too conservative. "Year by year, millimeter by millimeter, the seas are rising," he writes. "Fed by melting glaciers and ice sheets, and swollen by thermal expansion of water as the planet warms, the world's oceans now on average are about eight inches higher than a century ago. And this sea change is only getting started." Folger notes that eight of the world's ten largest cities are on seacoasts. Of course, rising sea levels will affect all of us, no matter where we live. At the same time, where we live will increasingly determine our quality of life. As Robert Kaplan puts it in his book *The Revenge of Geography* (2012), "The only enduring thing is a people's position on a map" (p. xviii).

According to the Conserve Energy Future website,

> The population of the planet is reaching unsustainable levels as it faces shortage of resources like water, fuel, and food. Population explosion in less developed and developing countries is straining the already scarce resources. Intensive agriculture practiced to produce food damages the environment through use of chemical fertilizer, pesticides and insecticides. Overpopulation is one of the crucial current environmental problems.

Clearly, respect for the Earth will become an integral part of every child's education, and students will learn to understand how their actions can contribute to solving rather than exacerbating our environmental plight.

Implications for the Formative Five. Empathy and embracing diversity will be very important, because many of the steps necessary to protect our environment will require us to make personal sacrifices in order to help others. We will look beyond our borders and take actions that we know will cost us in some way—though because we are all on the same planet, helping others is ultimately helping ourselves as well. Students will also need to develop self-control in making decisions that require staving off immediate gratification in exchange for a better future—and because environmental change is a complex problem with no easy solutions, tenacity and resilience—grit—will be necessary to make progress.

Contextual Prediction 2: Technology Will Touch Everything

As computer chips become ever smaller, faster, and more powerful, technology will become even more pervasive in our lives than it currently is. Ray Kurzweil "predicts that in the 2030s, human brains will be able to connect to the cloud, allowing us to send e-mails and photos directly to the brain and to back up our thoughts and memories. This will be possible, he says, via nanobots—tiny robots from DNA strands—swimming around in the capillaries of our brain" (Miles, 2015). Kurzweil refers here to an approaching singularity, with computers increasingly doing our problem solving for us with little human direction or intervention. (Bear in mind that intelligence *is* problem solving.) In a 2007 *New York Times* column titled "The Outsourced Brain," David Brooks makes the point succinctly: "'I had thought that the magic of the information age was that it allowed us to know more, but then I realized that the magic of the information age is that it allows us to know less."

Of course, the ubiquity of computers has already significantly changed how we work: we've gone from counting on fingers to using the abacus, slide rule, and adding machine to mostly observing as computations are done for us. We might analyze the problem, frame the question, and press a few buttons, but we know that computers are more accurate and infinitely faster than people at solving complex mathematical equations. Actually, scratch that—why waste time pressing buttons when you can just ask Siri for the answer?

Incredibly, Siri is *already* yesterday's technology. Today's computers can do more than just hear us; they can now go as far as to read our facial expressions and infer our emotions. It won't be too long until we're greeted at the hospital emergency room by computers—perhaps even holograms—that ask us our symptoms, observe our expressions and body language, and refer us to a specialist, accordingly. Indeed, a company called Affectiva, founded by Rana el Kaliouby, is already developing such an artificial intelligence. According to an article in *Fast Company* magazine, the company's technology "is sophisticated enough to distinguish smirks from smiles, or unhappy frowns from the empathetic pursing of lips" (Segran, 2015). How many receptionists or aides will be replaced by this kind of automation? (See el Kaliouby's 2015 TED Talk video for more information on Affectiva's work.)

Already, as pointed out by David Rotman (2013) in the *MIT Technology Review*, technology has had a major effect on employment. From nearly half of Americans working in agriculture in 1900, only 2 percent did so in 2000. Additionally, "The proportion of Americans employed in manufacturing has dropped from 30 percent in the post–World War II years to around 10 percent today—partly because of increasing automation, especially during the 1980s."

That is likely just the beginning. Rotman continues: a "less dramatic change, but one with a potentially far larger impact on employment, is taking place in clerical work and professional services. Technologies like the Web, artificial intelligence, big data, and improved analytics— all made possible by the ever increasing availability of cheap computing power and storage capacity—are automating many routine tasks." Claire Caine Miller captures the interplay between technology and jobs well in her *New York Times* article "As Robots Grow Smarter, American Workers Struggle to Keep Up" (2014); similarly, in *The Industries of the Future* (2016), Alec Ross warns that "tomorrow's labor market will be increasingly characterized by competition between humans and robots" (p. 247).

Sometimes I wonder about the potential consequences of the driverless car. Once we are able to sit comfortably in an automobile for long journeys without having to focus on the road, will we still need motels? How might driverless cars affect the airline and railroad industries? And as labor becomes increasingly automated, what will we do with our free time? According to Thomas Frey (2014), by "2030 the average person in the U.S. . . . will spend most of [his or her] leisure time on an activity that hasn't been invented yet" (p. 52).

That many jobs will be eliminated is beyond question. A 2016 article in *The Economist* notes that "a study published in 2013 by Carl Benedikt Frey and Michael Osborne of Oxford University stoked anxieties when it found that 47 percent of jobs in [the United States] were vulnerable to automation"—and that in poorer countries where jobs can more easily be automated, the percentages are even higher (e.g., 69 percent in India, 77 percent in China, and 85 percent in Ethiopia). As leadership guru Warren Bennis has memorably said, "The factory of the future will have only two employees, a man and a dog. The man will be there to feed the dog. The dog will be there to keep the man from touching the equipment."

Implications for the Formative Five: As we are freed more and more of mundane tasks and obligations, our ability to exert *self-control* and make wise choices will become ever more important. Increased opportunities to interact with those we do not know (only interacting online) mean that the attributes of *integrity* and *embracing diversity* will be particularly valuable.

Contextual Prediction 3: Diversity Will Be in Our Faces

As much as it pains me, I'm afraid that members of our species will continue to discriminate among one another. I would like to believe otherwise, but history is my guide—and recently, some of the responses to the Syrian refugee crisis and to terrorist acts by a few Muslims portend increased fear and discrimination throughout the West. And despite the United States' status as a melting pot, many Americans continue to struggle with diversity issues—unsurprisingly, given our history with slavery.

This legacy begins in 1619, when the first slaves were brought to North America from Africa. (In 2015, Andrew Kahn and Jamelle Bouie published a powerful video showing the paths of these forced journeys, which encompassed 20,528 slave ships over 315 years. You can see it here: www.slate.com/articles/life/the_history_of_american_slavery/2015/06 /animated_interactive_of_the_history_of_the_atlantic_slave_trade .html.) Indeed, from its very founding, the United States relied on slavery for much of its economy. Though it is rarely noted in history books, the founders paid a lot of attention to slavery when devising the Constitution. (Joseph Ellis's 2015 book *The Quartet* provides a wonderful summary of the deliberations and tensions between the northern and southern states during this "second American Revolution.")

In *Between the World and Me* (2015), Ta-Nehisi Coates notes that "at the onset of the Civil War," the "stolen bodies" of black slaves "were worth four billion dollars, more than all of American industry, all of American railroads, workshops, and factories combined, and the prime product rendered by our stolen bodies—cotton—was America's primary export" (p. 101). Although things have gotten much better, we have much more to do: Type *racial conflict* into Google's search engine and you'll get about 71,000,000 links. (*Ferguson shooting* results in about

34,200,000 links.) Our country will become even more diverse: according to estimates by the U.S. Census, "International migration will soon surpass natural increases (births minus deaths) as the principal driver of America's growth" (McGovern, 2016, p. 21). Looking ahead, it's clear that the speed and ease of communications technology will create exponentially more intersections among people of different races, religions, economic statuses, and beliefs.

Both technology and climate change will have enormous implications on diversity because disparities in living conditions will vary among groups even more in the future than they do today. Perhaps, generations from now, race will be a relic of the past. It's likely that practically all humans will one day be a salmagundi of different races. Even then, however, I fear that mankind will find other characteristics on the basis of which to discriminate.

Implications for the Formative Five: Interacting with others who are different than we are—whether in real time or online—will be virtually unavoidable, so *empathy* and *embracing diversity* will be even more central in the future than they are today. These same interactions will also require us to act with *integrity* to foster trust among one another.

The Future, in Education

Here are three predictions of changes related to education that I believe will have a profound effect on schools in the future—and that will point to the increasing importance of the Formative Five in curriculum and instruction.

Education Prediction 1: Educators Will Broaden Their Understanding of Student Growth, Thereby Expanding Their Responsibilities

In the future, appreciating the "whole child" will be the norm. Maslow was correct when he noted that we all need to have our basic needs met before we can fully focus on learning. Before we can help students with their self-actualization, we must meet their basic needs for safety, love, belonging, and esteem. Although meeting these needs is primarily the job of parents, we'd be naïve to think that it isn't part of our job as educators to address them. Consequently, I believe that future schools will provide more services intended to address the prerequisite needs of students.

Beyond ensuring students' health and safety, we will be emphasizing the Formative Five success skills more in the future. As we increasingly delegate lower-level tasks to machines, we will turn our focus to teaching students how to solve complex challenges by managing themselves (e.g., through *integrity, self-control,* and *grit*) and their relationships (e.g., by employing *empathy* and *embracing diversity*).

Higher-level problem solving, starting with determining the questions to be solved and the data to be used, will become more of a curricular and instructional focus in the future. I envision these areas being routinely assessed and discussed on students' report cards. (Having said this, and despite the high value that I place on the Formative Five, I am skeptical of the use of standardized testing to measure them well.)

Education Prediction 2: School Choice in Various Forms Will Be Standard and Will Have Major Implications on How Schools Are Organized

A myriad of school options for every student may seem inconceivable in a world where, historically, most students are assigned to schools according to where they live. But just as choices have proliferated in our everyday life, so too will they become increasingly central to education. Consider that it wasn't that long ago that the U.S. Postal Service was the only option for mailing a package, that we had just the three or four television channels to choose from, and that we had to hail cabs either by home phone or by standing on the corner. Even when our actual choices aren't that much greater, such as among commercial airline companies, we have access to more granular data and, consequently, more control of the process. (Remember when you had to call a travel agent to book a flight?)

I predict that a marketplace will arise that will enable families to select where and how their children should be educated. Up until recently, school choices have been available mostly to those who can afford them. Magnet and charter schools have begun to make choice more affordable (though chiefly in and around larger cities so far)—the number of charter schools has increased by 47 percent since 2007, and more than 6,400 of them were in operation in 2013 (Karp, 2013)—and I believe that the possibilities will only expand. It isn't hard to conceive that families will one day be able to select from a menu of educational options that includes their local public schools as well as charter, independent, religious, and for-profit choices.

Online learning opportunities are also bound to expand, allowing students living anywhere access to a mind-boggling number of courses. The Khan Academy is on the vanguard of this expansion, and I'm sure that a profusion of similar offerings will arise in time. It also won't be long until K–12 educators feel the effects of the massive, open, and online courses (MOOCs) that have already taken hold in the world of higher education: enrollment in post-secondary MOOCs doubled from 2011 to 2015, with 35 million students taking at least one. (I must note that I do not advocate using MOOCs especially with elementary-age students.)

A greater appreciation of what is required to be a successful adult coupled with more detailed data on students' specific needs will lead to more and more parents choosing "customized learning environments" for their children. I put the term in quotes because I don't believe that schools will *truly* be customized, but rather that different schools will have different focuses—and will market themselves accordingly. Dollars, whether in the form of tax revenues or tuition payments, are inextricably attached to students, so working to stand out in a competitive K–12 environment will be increasingly important. This shift to a more market-oriented approach will have profound repercussions on the way schools are organized and the behaviors that students and staffs are expected to value.

Consider, as an analogy, the restaurant business. Highly successful restaurants serve excellent-tasting food, sure, but that's only a part of the reason why they do well. Highly successful restaurants offer a narrow range of plates so they can focus on execution—and, more important, on providing customers with a pleasurable experience. Restaurateur Danny Meyer makes the point well in his book *Setting the Table* (2008):

> You may think, as I once did, that I'm primarily in the business of serving good food. Actually, though, food is secondary to something that matters even more. In the end, what's most meaningful is creating positive, uplifting outcomes for human experiences and human relationships. Business, like life, is all about how you make people feel. It's that simple, and it's that hard. (p. 3)

Similarly, I predict that in addition to providing a good education, schools of the future will pay more attention than they do today to creating positive relationships among their consumers (students) and customers (parents). (In fact, I refer to Meyer's point often in the principal preparation program in which I teach.)

Education Prediction 3: Technology Will Change How and What We Teach—and Will Make Diversity Increasingly Valuable

In the future, internet connectivity will be a given, and students will routinely work with handheld devices. Increased reliance upon screens in classrooms will make human interactions even more important than they are today. Teachers will find themselves working to develop teams within their classrooms to design activities that require students to interact "in the flesh." At the same time, students will find themselves interacting much more often with peers who live in other cities and countries. The working definition of a "classroom" will change as teachers routinely create settings for children from a range of backgrounds, living on different continents, to collaborate on solving common problems.

Of course, simply interacting with peers from different places and backgrounds won't automatically help students learn to respect and appreciate one another. Rather, skilled teachers will need to consciously work to develop these attitudes in their students, which will require them to adopt a new kind of mindset. As Carole Basile, dean of the

College of Education at the University of Missouri–St. Louis, puts it: "The expectations of a teacher have to shift. We would have developmental expectations for teachers and they would work in teams with groups of kids alongside socio-emotional experts" (personal communication, December 8, 2015).

Conclusion

Though the challenges confronting us may differ in many ways, their complexity requires collaborative solutions, with people of all kinds working together. Margaret Mead's famous quote—"Never doubt that a small group of thoughtful, committed citizens can change the world; indeed, it's the only thing that ever has"—is increasingly valid. These citizens may not live in the same neighborhood or even on the same continent, but they can be united in seeking solutions to common problems. *Empathy, self-control, integrity,* and *embracing diversity* will be key success skills as tomorrow's students and adults work and learn with and from others—and to solve all of the problems we will inevitably confront, we will need lots and lots of *grit.*

I fully expect—and encourage! —people wiser than I to disagree about my predictions. Of one point, however, I am certain: the Formative Five success skills will only become more important in schools as the years progress.

2

Empathy

Atticus was right. One time he said you never really know a man until you stand in his shoes and walk around in them. Just standing on the Radley porch was enough.

—Scout Finch in *To Kill a Mockingbird*

Katrina was consistent. No matter the situation and regardless of who was involved, things were always simple for her. She only ever saw things from her own perspective, unable to appreciate or even fathom others' points of view. Her narrow viewpoint provided her with a sense of security and comfort because she thought that everybody else shared it. Not surprisingly, Katrina's friendships did not last long, as others quickly tired of her rigidity. This never concerned her, though, as she immediately discounted anyone she felt wasn't in her corner.

Maurice was popular in large part because he seemed to care about everyone. He was a good listener, but it was more than that: he actually took the time to learn what others were saying and thinking. He understood the complexities of other people's situations and appreciated the challenges that they might pose—whether in school, discussing other cultures in World History, or in the community, serving meals at a homeless shelter on weekends. He was acutely aware of the disparity in resources available to his classmates, some of whom spent their vacations in Paris while others stayed home watching television. He was gracious in his judgments and tended to give others the benefit of the doubt. Maurice's teachers often told him that they thought he would be a great teacher.

Katrina and Maurice are archetypes, as are the other students profiled at the beginning of Chapters 3–6. Though it's unlikely that many students will suit each profile perfectly, we've all worked with students who lean more or less in a certain direction. By understanding our students not only as learners but as *people*, we can help them to successfully develop the attributes that they will need to thrive in the world beyond school.

In addition to student profiles, each of the chapters on the Formative Five success skills includes a self-assessment survey for teachers; I encourage you to take a moment and complete each one as you come to it. (Self-assessment surveys for students can be found in Appendix A.) Figure 2.1 shows the self-assessment survey for empathy.

What Is Empathy?

Collins English Dictionary defines *empathy* as "the psychological identification with or vicarious experiencing of the feelings, thoughts, or attitudes of another." In his book *Empathy* (2014), Roman Krznaric calls it "the art of stepping imaginatively into the shoes of [other people], understanding their feelings and perspectives, and using that understanding to guide your actions" (p. x)—and notes that empathy "is now acknowledged as an essential ingredient of well-being" (p. 34). There is an emotional aspect to empathy; it conveys feeling rather than an objective appraisal. In fact, the word itself is derived from the Greek *empatheia*, which roughly translates into "passion." As Jessica Lahey (2014) writes, "In order to be truly empathetic, children need to learn more than simple perspective-taking; they need to know how to value, respect and understand another person's views, even when they don't agree with them."

Although they sound alike, *empathy* and *sympathy* are quite different. We can sympathize with the plights of others without fully

FIGURE 2.1

Self-Assessment Survey: Empathy

Note: The following survey is designed to provide a sense of your feelings about empathy. It is a tool to elicit reflection and discussion, not a scientifically valid instrument.

Directions: Place a 1 (strongly disagree), 2 (disagree), 3 (not sure), 4 (agree), or 5 (strongly agree) after each item.

1. I raise a variety of different perspectives in class and ask students why people might share them. ___
2. Learning to see things from the perspectives of others is a practice best restricted to social or religious settings. ___
3. I occasionally share parts of my empathy journey with students (i.e., times when others have not considered how I felt and times when I have not considered the feelings of others). ___
4. Hearing a multitude of perspectives can be confusing to students. ___
5. In my personal life, I seek to hear the ideas of those who are different from me. ___
6. Students should be able to choose with whom to work and play. ___
7. It is most important for students to be comfortable with the perspectives of people like them. ___
8. Too much of an emphasis on relationships can detract from academics. ___
9. I ask students to identify what they have in common with people who see things differently than they do. ___
10. I assign readings by authors of different backgrounds and make a point of noting the difference to students. ___

Scoring:

___ (A) Total points for 1, 3, 5, 9, 10
___ (B) Total points for 2, 4, 6, 7, 8
___ (C) Subtract (B) from (A) for your "empathy" score

If you scored

- *18 or higher:* You fully understand the issue of empathy!
- *15–17:* You understand empathy but may need to work more directly on it with your students.
- *12–14:* You should probably focus more on empathy in your classroom instruction.
- *12 or lower:* You would probably benefit from reading up on or joining a discussion group about empathy.

Note: You can find an empathy self-assessment survey for students in Appendix A.

understanding—that is, empathizing with—their unique perspectives. As Lahey points out, because empathy is based on an interpersonal connection, it allows us to engage in deeper relationships with one another than mere sympathy does. Brené Brown captures the difference between the two sentiments well when she notes, "Empathy fuels connections, sympathy drives disconnection" (quoted in Heick, 2015).

Of course, it is essential for our empathy to be rooted in an *accurate* understanding of others' perspectives. Daniel Goleman (2006) notes that, to some, "empathic accuracy represents . . . *the* essential expertise in social intelligence" because it "builds on primal empathy but adds an explicit understanding of what someone else feels and thinks," and that a "deficit in such accuracy bodes poorly: one sign of a rockier relationship can be read when a partner realizes the other feels bad but has no clue as to what exactly might be on their mind" (pp. 88–89). True empathy begins with listening—taking the time not just to hear but to *understand* what someone else is thinking and feeling.

Why Start with Empathy?

There is a reason that I chose to begin our discussion of the Formative Five with a chapter devoted to empathy: as I have grown older, I have come to value its importance more and more. When I think about the qualities that I want in work colleagues, I realize that kindness and care are at the top of the list. Of course, knowledge, skills, and work ethic are incredibly important, but I spend a lot of time and invest a great deal of emotional energy at work, so I want to be able to trust and lean on the people around me.

The same is true of those with whom I spend my downtime. Whether it's during my Saturday morning basketball game, at my monthly book group, or when meeting a friend to solve the world's problems over coffee, I want to be around people who are kind and caring—who understand me and know how I am feeling. When I sense that kind of empathy, I feel more confident that we can develop a relationship based on real trust. Whether I'm hiring a new employee or inviting someone to join my book group, I always ask myself: "Is this person caring and kind?"

Why Do We Need Empathy?

There are wonderful teachers in every school, and while they vary in training and background, they all have one thing in common: *empathy*. To quote Homar Tavangar (2014), "Empathy is the most important back-to-school supply for teachers." Or as Carly Andrews, principal of Bosque Middle School in Albuquerque, New Mexico, says, "Empathy is central to great teaching and when it is lacking, ideas narrow, compassion wanes, and the great health of the teacher-family-child relational dynamic diminishes" (personal correspondence, January 27, 2016).

As we prepare our students for success beyond school, we need to understand that empathy is also an important business attribute. In a *New York Times* article about the hiring process, communications-service executive Stewart Butterfield makes the following observation:

> When we talk about the qualities we want in people, empathy is a big one. If you can empathize with people, then you can do a good job. If you have no ability to empathize, then it's difficult to give people feedback, and it's difficult to help people improve. Everything becomes harder. (Bryant, 2015)

In the absence of kindness and caring, relationships are destined to fail. In his classic article "Social Behavior as Exchange," George Homans (1958) points out that we remain in relationships because of what we derive from them, whether tangible (e.g., money or skills) or intangible (e.g., the pleasure of another's company). As long as our gains exceed our costs, we are content. Luckily, interpersonal relationships are not zero-sum; in fact, the more each party gains from one, the stronger the relationship becomes! As Brené Brown says in her book *Rising Strong* (2015), "When you practice empathy and compassion with someone, there [aren't fewer] of these qualities to go around"; there are more (p. 392).

(Though it may sometimes appear as though people choose to stay in harmful relationships against their better interests, many of them feel that the cost of cutting ties would be even worse than that of staying.)

From the Crusades to slavery to the Holocaust, the history of humankind is littered with examples of a mass lack of empathy resulting in cruelty to others and the persecution of different groups. Without empathy, we tend to divide people into "us" and "them," which leads to suspicion, miscommunication, and conflict. Bullying results from a lack of empathy, and its consequences can be long-lasting: adults with misanthropic tendencies are likely to have been bullied or taken advantage of as children. As Daniel Goleman (1995) notes, one "psychological fault line is common to rapists, child molesters, and many perpetrators of family violence alike: they are incapable of empathy" (p. 106).

Experiments in Empathy

In addition to seeing the world through an "us-versus-them" lens, strict adherence to authority and a desire to satisfy a peer group—to go along to get along—can lead to a marked reduction in sensitivity to the plight of others. Stanley Milgram's landmark "Behavioral Study of Obedience" (1963) proved this point rather chillingly. For his study, Milgram recruited white male volunteers aged 25 to 50 to take part in an experiment in which they were to play the role of "teacher" and follow the directions of a man wearing a gray technician's coat. The man told the volunteers to inflict electric shocks on a "learner" (actually an actor) positioned behind a wall, ostensibly to determine the effects of the shocks on learning; the more supposed mistakes the "learner" made on his unspecified assignment, the stronger the shocks the recruits were to administer. As the experiment wore on, the volunteers were asked to inflict increasingly painful levels of voltage to the "learner," and they complied time after time, despite the anguished cries of pain from the other side of the wall—simply because an authority figure had exhorted them to do so.

Milgram's findings are dramatic and disturbing. Twenty-six of the 40 "teachers" in the initial experiment went far beyond what we would expect and hope, and administered the maximum possible voltage to the "learners." Though many of them expressed unease, they continued to inflict shocks regardless. But why?

I believe that an absence of empathy for the "learner" contributed to the cruelty of the "teachers" in Milgram's experiment. If the volunteers had felt real empathy for the person on the other side of the wall, they wouldn't have been willing to inflict so much pain. Of course, Milgram's experiment was designed to limit empathy: The "teachers" and "learners" did not know one another, did not interact other than to inflict and receive shocks, and were separated by a wall—and the instructor, who wore a technician's coat to reinforce his authority, did not offer the "teachers" the option of stopping.

The notorious 1971 Stanford Prison Experiment (Zimbardo, 2016), in which college students were divided into "prisoners" and "guards," similarly revealed just how precarious our sense of empathy can be. The hostility and cruelty that the "guards" displayed to the "prisoners," whom they had previously seen as equals, was intense and painful to watch. In taking on their roles of authority, the "guards" quickly lost their ability to empathize with "prisoners."

Another well-known experiment that addresses empathy is Jane Elliott's famous "Blue Eyes/Brown Eyes" exercise, which Elliott designed to teach her 3rd graders about discrimination (2006). During the experiment, she asked her students to discriminate against their classmates based on the color of their eyes—and they proved only too happy to do so, reflecting a lack of empathy for those who suffer discrimination.

Unfortunately, lack of empathy and consequent displays of cruelty are not confined to psychological experiments. Perhaps, as Maya Angelou once said, "I think we all have empathy. We may not have enough courage to display it" at all times (Murphy, 2013).

Empathy in the 21st Century

It's human nature for us to retreat to our tribes and to feel most comfortable among those who look, act, and think like us. The ongoing technology explosion only makes this kind of balkanization easier. Consider that it wasn't that long ago that Americans had a choice of a few national television channels to watch, resulting in a relatively homogenized culture. Today, we have so many media sources that it's all too easy to tune in only to those that reinforce our preexisting biases. A Kaiser Family Foundation study notes that "eight- to eighteen-year-olds spend more time with media than in any other activity besides (maybe) sleeping—an average of more than 7½ hours a day, seven days a week" (2010, p. 1).

According to Sherry Turkle (2015), face-to-face conversation is "where we develop the capacity for empathy" (p. 5), so not it's not surprising that "technology is implicated in an assault on empathy" (p. 6). Indeed, the plethora of personal information about people available to all of us in a matter of keystrokes makes it all the easier to select only those whose information matches ours as friends. The opportunities for self-selection on this scale mean that we interact less with those whose viewpoints we don't share, thus making it harder for us to understand and feel empathy to them. Daniel Goleman (2006) quotes Preston and de Waal as saying that "in today's era of e-mail, commuting, frequent moves, and bedroom communities, the scales are increasingly tipped against the automatic and accurate perception of others' emotional state, without which empathy is impossible" (p. 62). Goleman further says that "modern-day social and virtual distances have created an anomaly in human living, though one we now take to be the norm. This separation mutes empathy, absent which altruism falters" (p. 62). Unless our students become hermits or lighthouse keepers, chances are that they will be working with other people in the future. Building and sustaining relationships will be a key to their success—and empathy will be at the root of their ability to do this.

Goleman (2006) observes that empathy begins with listening and understanding, and that "listening well has been found to distinguish the best managers, teachers, and leaders" (p. 88). Truly, listening is the most important leadership skill. Listening is more than hearing; it is taking the time to understand and think about what the other person is saying.

I used to have a poster hanging in my office that said "Life is curvilinear"—meaning that too much of a good thing can end up being a bad thing. An excess of empathy can lead to feelings of guilt, angst, or even depression. Indeed, the term "compassion fatigue" is sometimes applied to people who give so much of themselves to others that they soon deplete their emotional reservoirs.

Though we need to be aware of this danger, I'm not too worried. Society *needs* more empathy. Then-senator Barack Obama drove the point home well in a commencement speech to the 2006 graduating class of Northwestern University:

> There's a lot of talk in this country about the federal deficit. But I think we should talk more about our empathy deficit— the ability to put ourselves in someone else's shoes; to see the world through those who are different from us—the child who's hungry, the laid-off steelworker, the immigrant woman cleaning your dorm room.
>
> As you go on in life, cultivating this quality of empathy will become harder, not easier. There's no community service requirement in the real world; no one forcing you to care. You'll be free to live in neighborhoods with people who are exactly like yourself, and send your kids to the same schools, and narrow your concerns to what's going in your own little circle.
>
> Not only that—we live in a culture that discourages empathy. A culture that too often tells us our principal goal in life is to be rich, thin, young, famous, safe, and entertained. A culture where those in power too often encourage these selfish impulses.

The Steps to Developing Empathy

We need to teach empathy to students the same way we would approach teaching them any other skill: by valuing a commitment to growth. No matter how well we may know a skill, there's always room for improvement by way of focus, effort, and reflection. There are six basic steps to developing empathy:

1. Listening
2. Understanding
3. Internalizing
4. Projecting
5. Planning
6. Intervening

The first two steps—listening and understanding—constitute *awareness*: Students must first pay attention to others and then take the time to learn what is being said and how (and for more mature students, perceiving what *isn't* being said). Understanding doesn't necessarily mean agreeing; it simply means having a cognitive grasp of another person's views.

Perhaps the most difficult step in helping students develop empathy is teaching them to internalize what they have learned. To place themselves in other people's shoes and actually *experience* their feelings—now that's empathy! Projecting is the next step, when students are able to imagine how they would react in the same situation. They can also work to imagine how the perceptions that they hold are perceived by others, and appreciate how easy or difficult that might be for the other person. Together, these opening steps lead students to appreciate how easy or difficult it might be to be someone else in a different context.

Once students have developed empathy, the next step is to create a context for collaborative effort. In step five, students are able to plan a response to a given situation informed by their empathy—perhaps starting with conversations toward common understanding and respect, or attempts to alter the situation, or both—and in step six, they execute their plan. Planning should always be inclusive and collaborative: successful change doesn't come from what we do to or for others, but rather from what we do together.

Each of the Formative Five success skills is best learned actively, by doing. This is particularly true for empathy and embracing diversity, interpersonal skills that we derive by considering and interacting with others. As Krznaric (2014) says, "It is by stepping into the world of experience—through immersions, exploration, and cooperation—that we can make huge leaps in our ability to understand the lives of others" (p. 96).

To develop success skills in our students, we must first develop them in ourselves. We'll never be perfect, and neither will our students, but we do need to be role models—and we must model not only values and skills but also the thoughtful and transparent pursuit of them. We need to consider virtually every interaction as a potential teaching opportunity. "In our educational roles, it is vitally important that we model how empathy has power to influence a variety of contexts and interactions," note Crowley and Saide (2016). Our students need to know that we are all on the same journey—that although we are at different places and making progress at different speeds, we all aspire to the same goals. In this case, we need to consciously step outside of our backgrounds and situations—just as we expect our students to do—and work to understand others.

Strategies for Developing Empathy

For all teachers:

• **Help students recognize and understand the perspectives of others.** Discussions on current events, history, or literature are excellent starting points, though the "others" we are working to understand can also include fellow students. Remember: empathy begins with listening and trying to understand. We need to continually emphasize—teach— this sequence to our students.

• **Have students engage in service learning.** Collecting blankets for the local animal shelter, planting and tending to crops for a food bank, and preparing food at a homeless shelter are good examples of service learning experiences that can help to engender empathy in students. (We have done all three at my school.) It's always best to tie altruism to an aspect of curriculum (e.g., related to a book from English class or a topic in social studies).

• **Help students appreciate their own backgrounds and biases.** Ask students to answer the question "Why am I the way I am?" by interviewing relatives, researching family histories, and creating self-presentations that feature music and photos and cover a range of information (e.g., geographic locations, ethnicity, family size, religion). The presentations can serve as a rich resource for teachers and students, as another way to understand some "others." (The data could be tallied and analyzed as a logical-mathematical activity, too.)

- **Create safe spaces for students to tell their stories.** It's one thing to read about the experiences of strangers or fictional characters; it's far more powerful to hear stories from people we know. Helping students to frame and share their personal difficulties with one another can help them to drive appreciation and empathy. As the Forum for Youth Investment states, "Telling and responding to someone's story plays out as part of a service learning activity, such as planting a garden in memory of someone who lost their life to a drunk driver" (Smith, McGovern, Larson, Hillaker, & Peck, 2016, p. 56).

- **Consciously teach about stereotypes and discrimination, the history and evolution of attitudes, and the reasons why people's degrees of empathy toward different people vary.** From the Crusades and Westward Expansion to the subjugation of blacks, Jews, and women, there is no lack of fodder. Ask "What caused some groups or individuals to be so insensitive to the needs of others?" Remind students that the goal is not to empathize in all cases with everyone, but rather to act kindly whether or not you do.

- **Have students examine historical examples of innocent people who were wrongly accused of crimes.** Study the trial of Galileo, the Salem Witch Trials, or the Dreyfus Affair. The goal is to help students see the perspectives not only of the wrongly accused but also of the other characters involved. It may be easy to feel empathy for the protagonist, so it is important for students to see the interplay of perspectives so that they can speculate on which other character(s) might warrant their sympathy or empathy. (Arthur Miller's *The Crucible*, about the Salem Witch Trials, is a very powerful—and fairly short—resource.) Then ask your students to reflect on a time when they were wrongly accused of some misdeed. Have them generate adjectives and drawings or perhaps a song or dance to capture how they felt and how others in the situation felt, too.

• **Always encourage students to consider situations from a variety of perspectives.** We want our students to feel empathy for those who are not the same as they are. "How might someone see that differently?" may elicit a good discussion. Although being able to identify and understand different perspectives does not guarantee empathy, it is a starting point.

• **Assign books that feature a diversity of humanity.** It's especially worthwhile to choose works that feature ethnic or other groups under-represented in the school.

• **Create a system by which students can submit anonymous compliments for specific classmates.** Then, quietly or publicly, pass along the praise. The goal here is to help students understand what others might appreciate, particularly how others might appreciate something that is not particularly meaningful to them.

• **Get students involved in charitable causes.** This is a good way to highlight the differences between empathy and sympathy. For example, a retired librarian from the Shelburne Community School in Vermont, Ellen Matthews (in a personal communication on February 8, 2016), reports that a kindergarten teacher at her school had students raise money by selling plants they grew in class to fund projects they found on the website for Kiva (www.kiva.org), an organization that makes small loans to people around the world. Fourth and 5th grade students fundraised and collected donated items that they took to Burlington's organization and shelter for the homeless. While there, students talked to residents and counselors and learned about the people, their challenges, and ways that they could help.

For middle and high school teachers,

• **Teach students about the differences in perspective between journalism and literature and between current and historical accounts.** As Deb Holmes, former assistant superintendent of the Kirkwood (Missouri) School District, says, "It is difficult for one to have empathy without considering the possibility that one's perspective is not the only perspective" (personal communication, October 11, 2015). Use assigned readings to help students see various perspectives and distinguish between empathy and sympathy. Books such as Charles Dickens's *A Tale of Two Cities* (1859/1999), Lois Lowry's *The Giver* (1993), and John Steinbeck's *The Grapes of Wrath* (1939) provide enough characters and complexity to generate good thought and discussion. Consider the wise words of Barbara Kingsolver: "Good fiction creates empathy. A novel takes you somewhere and asks you to look through the eyes of another person, to live another life" (Jaggi, 2010).

   • **Invite speakers who can give "the story behind the headlines."** Homeless people, veterans with post-traumatic stress disorder, undocumented immigrants: any number of categories of individuals can tell their unique stories to help students develop empathy. These interactions help us to understand others as more than caricatures or stereotypes. Teachers need to be explicit about the goal—to help students reflect on and better understand why they think and see things the way they do—while also noting that not everyone will necessarily arrive at true empathy.

   • **Read portions of Paul Theroux's book *Deep South* (2015) with students to examine a slice of life with which they may not be familiar.** The book follows Theroux as he visits with good people who are grappling with the effects of globalization and—even today—the long-term vestiges of slavery.

   • **Draw content from *Material World: A Global Family Portrait* (1995) by Peter Menzel and Charles Mann.** This book features photos of families from around the world posing next to their homes with all of their possessions. It provides a quick and dramatic window into the differences in wealth among families—while also making the point that wealth isn't necessary for happiness. It's important for children to see beyond economic disparities if they are to understand this point. Depending upon the age of students, ask them,

   o Why do you think each family has so much (or so little)?

   o What is the difference between a *need* and a *want*? Does the same answer apply to everyone in all cultures?

   o By category (e.g., electronics, furniture, clothing), what are some of the disparities among the families' possessions?

○ How might climate affect what a family has or needs?

○ Do any of the families appear to be in jeopardy?

○ Based on the photos, what activities might be difficult for some of the families?

○ Can you find items that a particular family may not need? Does your family have things that it doesn't need?

○ What might people from other families think that we need or do not need?

These analyses can also lend themselves to teaching the differences among mean, median, and mode. (A similar book by the same authors, *Hungry Planet: What the World Eats* [2005], can be used the same way.)

For elementary school teachers:

• **Teach students the difference between sympathy and empathy.** It may help to present empathy as the highest level on a three-step developmental sequence, with sympathy as step two and step one being care (i.e., the positive feelings we might have toward a pet).

• **Use empathy as a tool to help students understand character creation and development in fiction.** When we find our attention seized by a story—such as by Harper Lee's *To Kill a Mockingbird* (1960) or Raquel J. Palacio's *Wonder* (2012)—it's because we reach beyond sympathy to empathize with the characters. Students should consider how the author causes us to feel empathy for some characters and not others.

• **Use games and competitions to help students see situations from others' perspectives.** Remind students that though we all want to win, we're bound to lose sometimes—and we should remember how losing feels when we do win. Open up the discussion by having students share times when they felt the sting of a loss. Laurie Falk, counselor at New City School in St. Louis, Missouri, notes that the goal in these situations should be to enable students to empathize on their own, without adult prodding (personal communication, December 14, 2015).

• **Ask students to speculate as to what other children might like to receive for their birthdays—discounting what they might want for themselves.** Consider using this exercise to conclude a discussion of the different interests among students' family members. The goal here is for the children to learn to step out of their perspectives and work to see how others feel.

• **If a student's pet dies, use the occasion to talk about feelings.** Many students will naturally feel empathy in this situation with the student whose pet died.

For principals:

• **Make it a priority to hire teachers who are empathetic toward all kinds of students—not just those who excel in school and are well-behaved.** Teacher candidates should be able to explain how they might identify and care for students in a variety of situations. When interviewing, I often ask teachers to describe a time when they had to respond to a student who was having difficulties or to tell me how they might intervene in a hypothetical situation. My goal is less to learn more about the specific strategies they might use and more to determine how much of an effort they would make to know and understand their students.

Similarly, Mark Catalana, director of human resources for the Mehlville (Missouri) School District, asks teacher applicants to describe an occasion when they learned about a student going through a difficult time, and then asks them whether that knowledge changed the way they treated the student. He explains his rationale: "By having empathy, we show a humanistic side of us. I also encourage teachers to open up with those students (without getting too personal) by sharing some of their hurdles they experienced in their life" (personal communication, January 26, 2016).

Sometimes Mark also asks applicants to tell them about any personal struggles they had as children. How did they handle them? Did it affect their schooling? Did anyone in the school help them get through their difficulties? According to Mark, applicants are often puzzled at his line of questioning. "I explain to them that over their careers, at least one child every year in their classroom will go through a personal struggle," he said. "These students won't always come and tell you about it, though. It's up to you as a teacher to look for changes in behavior, social-ization, and academics in order to identify those kids. By having empa-thy, we show a humanistic side of us."

• **Work to help teachers appreciate their students' home and com-munity environments.** It's natural for teachers to view students through the prism of mathematics or literature or biology, but such a narrow viewpoint reduces the teacher's empathy for students. At the begin-ning of every school year and after every school break, teachers should structure in some class time to hear from their students so that they can better understand them. (Although there is never enough time to cover all of our curriculum, this is an investment in the relationship and the student.) In addition to providing teachers with valuable insights into their students' lives, this exercise is a great way to model the kinds of listening that we want students to adopt. Short, one-on-one meetings with students during which they're asked to describe events that sur-prised them when they were away from school can elicit particularly rich reports and enhance teacher-student rapport. (I like asking about surprises rather than "good" or "bad" events to give students a broader choice of answers.)

• **Sponsor an "Empathy Night" such as the one at Killip Elemen-tary School in Flagstaff, Arizona.** There, "students performed songs about love and kindness, and students from the martial arts program displayed some of their techniques. The school also had a food dona-tion box to collect for the food bank, and students made cards for resi-dents at The Peaks Senior Living Community" (Vanek, 2015).

• **Create a "Social Action Committee" among faculty to help students (and possibly parents) make a difference in the commu-nity.** From singing at a retirement home to assembling sandwiches at a homeless shelter to picking up litter around the school, opportunities for students of all ages to contribute abound. A good first step is to have students create a matrix of community needs and develop a set of crite-ria to which they can be aligned. This exercise should provide students with a better and broader understanding of their community's needs and resources—and of how they personally can make a difference.

• **Screen Brené Brown's two-minute documentary,** *Brené Brown on Empathy* **(2013).** Ginny Fendell, director of health and wellness for Whitfield School in St. Louis, Missouri, says that she shows the documentary for high school students every year and it always elicits a thoughtful discussion. I would first screen the video for faculty and then ask teachers to meet in groups and discuss how it resonated with them personally and how they might discuss it with students.

• **Form a voluntary faculty book group to read books related to empathy.** Ensuring total transparency of the selection process, choose books such as *Daring Greatly* (2012) and *Rising Strong* (2015), both by Brené Brown; *Ghettoside* (2015), by Jill Leovy; and *High Price* (2014), by Carl Hart. All of these are compelling works that enable us to see difficult situations from the perspectives of others.

Books That Support the Development of Empathy

Picture books:

- *Chrysanthemum* (1991), by Kevin Henkes
- *First-Grade Dropout* (2015), by Audrey Vernick and Matthew Cordell
- *How to Heal a Broken Wing* (2008), by Bob Graham
- *The Invisible Boy* (2013), by Trudy Ludwig and Patrice Barton
- *The Mitten Tree* (2009), by Candace Christiansen and Elaine Greenstein
- *The Sneetches and Other Stories* (1961), by Dr. Seuss
- *Unicorn Thinks He's Pretty Great* (2013), by Bob Shea
- *Beatrice's Goat* (2004), by Page McBrier and Lori Lohstoeter

Chapter books:

- *El Deafo* (2014), by Cece Bell
- *Have You Filled a Bucket Today: A Guide to Daily Happiness for Kids* (2006), by Carol McCloud and David Messing
- *Seedfolks* (1997), by Paul Fleischman

- *The Seventh Most Important Thing* (2015), by Shelley Pearsall
- *Stand in My Shoes: Kids Learning About Empathy* (2013), by Bob Sornson
- *When I Care About Others* (2002), by Cornelia Maude Spelman and Kathy Parkinson
- *Wonder* (2012), by Raquel J. Palacio

3

Self-Control

I generally avoid temptation unless I can't resist it.

—Mae West

KAPOW!!! BANG!! BANG!! BANG!! KAPOW!!!

The explosion of firecrackers rang through the quiet neighborhood on a Sunday evening. Tom had thrown them into the mail slot at his girlfriend's house before taking off running. He didn't anticipate that his girlfriend's dad would angrily confront him a couple of minutes later. "It seemed like a good idea at the time" was the only weak response Tom could muster. His girlfriend's dad was astonished—prior to seeing Tom run across the street, he thought that he was a reasonably intelligent high school sophomore who possessed some degree of self-control. He could see now that he was wrong.

Carla was a responsible overachiever. She knew what she needed to do, did it, and then checked it—often more than once. In elementary school, she was always sure to finish her homework before going outside to play, and she placed her folder by her door key each night so that she would remember to take it to school. In high school, Carla did not engage in many extracurricular activities because her priority was preparing to one day attend medical school. Today Carla is a successful physician and continues to remain always aware of and in control of her emotions. Her colleagues know that they can depend on her to get tough jobs done because of how well she is able to focus.

In the above examples, Tom clearly needs more self-control, and Carla could probably do with a bit less. An overabundance of self-control can inhibit us from taking risks, being extemporaneous, and generally enjoying life. Finding the balance is the key. (By the way, unlike the other archetypes in this book, Tom is actually a real person—in fact, he is the author of this book. Yep, it happened, and, yep, as I told my girlfriend's dad, "It seemed like a good idea at the time.")

Figure 3.1 shows the self-assessment survey for *self-control*. Take a moment to answer the questions before continuing with this chapter.

What Is Self-Control?

Daniel Goleman (1995) defines self-control as "the ability to modulate and control one's actions in age-appropriate ways; a sense of inner-control" (p. 194); Walter Mischel (2014) says it is "the ability to delay gratification and resist temptation" (p. 6). Some level of self-control is necessary for achieving success in every domain.

Self-control is as elusive as it is important. The importance is evidenced by the persistent panoply of self-help books on the best seller list year after year. Its elusiveness is illustrated in the fact that, according to Statistic Brain (n.d.), 67 percent of all people with gym memberships never use them. (I'll be sure to check on this the next time I go to the gym—whenever that happens.) Although he doesn't explicitly use the term, economist James Heckman (2013) makes clear its importance when discussing success in life, noting that self-control "depends upon much more than smarts. Non-cognitive abilities—including strength of motivation, an ability to act on long-term plans, and the social-emotional regulation needed to work with others—also have a large impact on earnings, employment, labor force experience, college attendance, teenage pregnancy, participation in risky activities, compliance with health protocols, and participation in crime" (p. 12).

FIGURE 3.1

Self-Assessment Survey: Self-Control

Note: The following survey is designed to provide a sense of your feelings about self-control. It is a tool to elicit reflection and discussion, not a scientifically valid instrument.

Directions: Place a 1 (strongly disagree), 2 (disagree), 3 (not sure), 4 (agree), or 5 (strongly agree) after each item.

1. Self-control is a part of personality; students either have it or they don't. ___
2. If students work hard and do well, self-control will develop. ___
3. Self-control can be improved. ___
4. Giving students choices has no effect on their self-control. ___
5. It's important to be aware of the issues that make self-control hard. ___
6. Self-control in one area can lead to developing it in another area. ___
7. Having self-control means not being spontaneous or creative. ___
8. Student self-control should be a focus of parents, not educators. ___
9. Students can support peers' efforts to develop self-control. ___
10. Setting self-control goals for behaviors outside of school can positively affect self-control goals for behaviors in school. ___

Scoring:

___ (A) Total points for questions 3, 5, 6, 9, 10

___ (B) Total points for questions 1, 2, 4, 7, 8

___ (C) Subtract (B) from (A) for your "self-control" score

If you scored

- *18 or higher:* You fully understand the issue of self-control!
- *15–17:* You understand self-control but may need to work more directly on it with your students.
- *12–14:* You should probably focus more on self-control in your classroom instruction.
- *11 or lower:* You would probably benefit from reading up on or joining a discussion group about self-control.

Note: You can find a self-control self-assessment survey for students in Appendix A.

Of course, educators spend a lot of time and energy helping students develop self-control (though like Heckman, we may not always use the term). Just about every classroom has a few students (and maybe more) whose performance suffers due to a lack of this essential skill. Not doing homework, falling short of expectations, being distracted in class, failing to study—too often, students aren't disciplined enough to consistently manage themselves.

The most famous study on self-control is the Stanford marshmallow experiment, colloquially known as the Marshmallow Test, first conducted by Walter Mischel at Stanford University in 1960 (Mischel, 2014). Here's how the experiment works: One at a time, 4-year-old children sit in a room alone with an adult researcher. The researcher offers each of the children a marshmallow and tells them that they can either eat it immediately or wait 15 minutes and receive a second marshmallow as a reward for their patience. The researcher then leaves the child alone in the room with the marshmallow. Can you imagine the temptation that these young children felt?

In Mischel's initial study, results were mixed: some of the children ate the marshmallow immediately and others waited the e-n-t-i-r-e 15 minutes so that they could receive another marshmallow. At age 4, there were already differences in the degree of self-control that children possess. But that is just the beginning. Over time, Mischel and his researchers saw that the decision about eating the marshmallow at age 4 suggested a trajectory about individuals' self-control that continued to play out throughout later life:

• "The more seconds they waited at age four or five, the higher their SAT scores and the better their rated social and cognitive functioning in adolescence. At age 27–32, those who had waited longer during the Marshmallow Test in preschool had a lower body mass index and a better sense of self-worth, pursued their goals more effectively, and coped more adaptively with frustration and stress" (p. 5).

• "Preschoolers who delayed longer on the Marshmallow Test were rated a dozen years later to be adolescents who exhibited more control in frustrating situations; yielded less to temptation; were less distractible when trying to concentrate; were more intelligent, self-reliant, and confident; trusted their own judgment. When under stress they did not go to pieces as much as the low delayers did, and they were less likely to become rattled and disorganized or revert to immature behavior. Likewise, they thought ahead and planned more, and when motivated they were able to pursue their goals. They were also more attentive and able to use and respond to reason, and they were less likely to be sidetracked by setbacks. In short, they managed to defy the widespread stereotype of the problematic, difficult adolescent, at least in the eyes of their parents and teachers" (pp. 23–24).

- "Around age twenty-five to thirty, those who had delayed longer in preschool self-reported that they were more able to pursue and reach long-term goals, used risky drugs less, had reached higher educational levels, and had a significantly lower body mass index. They were also more resilient and adaptive in coping with interpersonal problems and better at maintaining close relationships" (pp. 24–25).

The power of Mischel's work stems from the fact that a simple experiment gives insight into children's ability to exert self-control at an early age, and this has implications for later life. That said, we must look at the experiment carefully (as we should with all experiments). To what degree, we should ask, might the children's backgrounds influence their decision making? A child who has learned not to trust adults, for example, might wisely be prone to not believe an adult's promise of a second marshmallow. In fact, Mischel refers to this possibility, noting that "there's no good reason for anyone to forgo the 'now' unless there is trust that the 'later' will materialize" (p. 72). A child who has been without food for some time might also choose to eat the marshmallow immediately. Too, in a 2010 *Daily Beast* article, Po Bronson and Ashley Merryman articulated some criticisms of the Marshmallow Test, suggesting that the group of students wasn't large enough for a statistically valid result. In my mind, even if these concerns are just, the point remains that self-control is present at an early age in some children, and the limited data suggest that this correlates with positive behaviors throughout life.

As a child, how good were *you* at delaying gratification? In 5th grade, did you do your homework before or after playing outside or chatting on the phone? In high school, did you devote enough energy to your studies, or were you more concerned with hanging out or playing on your computer? Today, are you able to focus your time, attention, and effort on what's important despite any distractions? (Is your mind wandering now???)

The degree to which we are able to maintain self-control is especially important when we're bothered about something. "From the parent who gets upset with the teacher and instantly yanks her child out of that school, to the CEO who gets cold feet because of some bad numbers and changes strategies without thinking through their implications, the ability to control your thinking when your emotions are enflamed is huge for success," notes Henry Cloud (2006, p. 130). Paul Tough describes how this can happen with students: "Talking back and acting up in class are, at least in part, symptoms of a child's inability to control impulses, de-escalate confrontations, and manage anger and other strong feelings . . ." (2016, p. 55).

As we get older, temptations may change, but they never disappear. The good news is that self-control can be taught: as Charles Duhigg (2012) says in *The Power of Habit*, "Willpower is a learnable skill, something that can be taught the same way kids learn to do math and say 'thank you'" (p. 134). And of course, *willpower* is just another word for self-control. Our executive function—that "set of mental skills that help you get things done" ("Executive Function Skills and Disorders," 2016)—relies heavily on self-control. According to Kaufman (2010), both impulse control and emotional control are important aspects of the executive function's "social-emotional regulation strand" (p. 5). The perils of insufficient self-control are clear: "Because individuals lacking in self-control are insensitive to others and are risk-taking, they are also more likely to experience problems in social relationships, such as marriage, they are more likely to use drugs and to abuse alcohol, and they are more likely not to wear a seat belt and to get into automobile accidents" (Wright, 2009).

Malcolm Gladwell's famous "10,000-hour rule" (2008) is a good example of how important self-control is to success in all endeavors. To illustrate the rule, Gladwell discusses the fact that the Beatles' "overnight success" was actually 20 years in the making. What opportunities did John, Paul, George, and Ringo give up to pursue their passion? How many distractions must they have resisted? (Of course, spending 10,000 hours on something won't matter much without a baseline of talent. I could spend far more than 10,000 hours shooting baskets, for example, and I still wouldn't be as good as I'd like.)

The good news is that regardless of whether or not we ate the marshmallow, we can always improve. As Mischel (2014) says, "Beginning early in life, some people are better than others at self-control, but almost everybody can find ways to make it easier" (p. 12). And humans have always had trouble resisting temptation—just think how different things would be without Adam and Eve and the concept of forbidden fruit. Or consider Ulysses, who had his sailors shackle him to the mast of his ship so that he wouldn't be lured by the songs of the Sirens in the Aegean Sea. Impulse control is a recurring theme throughout history and literature for a reason: it reflects a constant preoccupation.

As we all know, technology has exponentially multiplied the number of distractions in our daily lives. It's gotten so bad that Apple now offers a free app called SelfControl that "lets you block your own access to distracting websites, your mail servers, or anything else on the internet. Just set a period of time to block for, add sites to your blacklist, and click 'Start.' Until that timer expires, you will be unable to access those sites—even if you restart your computer or delete the application" (SelfControl, n.d.; see www.selfcontrolapp.com for more information).

Hopefully we can help our students develop enough self-control not to need an app to filter online distractions. As David Brooks (2011) says, "There is no questioning self-control is one of the essential ingredients of a fulfilling life" (p. 123). It's actually easier to develop self-control as we age (so there is still hope for me!). Mischel (2014) notes, "Most children younger than four are unable to sustain delay of gratification on the Marshmallow Test. When faced with temptations, they ring the bell or start nibbling on the treats within about 30 seconds. . . . In contrast, by age 12 almost 60 percent of children in some studies have been able to wait as long as 25 minutes, a very long time to be sitting facing a few cookies and a bell in a barren room" (p. 47).

According to Mark Muraven, "Willpower isn't just a skill. It's a muscle, like the muscles in your arms or legs, and it gets tired as it works harder, so there's less power left over for other things" (quoted in Duhigg, 2012, p. 137). If we want students to develop and flex their self-control muscles, we must present them with (somewhat limited) choices so that they can learn to take responsibility for their behaviors while we stand back (even if it means gritting our teeth). Children must learn to consider alternatives, make a decision, and accept the consequences. Of course, these consequences may be difficult or even painful for students, so we must guide them, without shielding them, in a spirit of care.

Candidly, it can be easier to work with children when they are allowed no discretion and the path to approval is as clear as the penalties are obvious. But although this approach may be easier for adults, it doesn't benefit the children.

An example from my days as an elementary principal is instructive. One November I was talking with Arnie, a friend who was the assistant principal at the district's middle school, where he spent most of his time disciplining students for misbehavior.

"How is Marty doing?" I asked. Marty had been my single most challenging student the previous year. When he responded that he'd never met Marty and didn't even know who he was, I was shocked. I knew for a fact that Marty was attending his school. How can this be, I wondered? After all, Marty and I were regular acquaintances because he used to get sent to my office once or twice a week. He was a good kid, but he could be rude and he wasn't terribly motivated to follow school rules. Marty didn't have much self-control.

I followed up by asking Arnie about some other students now attending his school—Janel, Alan, and Pete—all three of whom were also frequent visitors to my office in elementary school. He didn't know any of them! Arnie told me that he wasn't surprised that he hadn't met these students yet because the most challenging kids at his school came from a different elementary school in the district—one known for being a "tight ship" with a culture of very strict discipline. The principal of this school took pride in its extraordinarily quiet halls and the orderly lines of students heading from class to class. (When I went to the school once for an administrative meeting, I actually found myself whispering so that I wouldn't get in trouble!) According to Arnie, these students were never given choices, so they had a particularly difficult time behaving themselves when they went to a larger and more fluid middle-school situation. The elementary school that those students attended was so rules-oriented and constricting that they had never had the opportunity to develop self-control. (However, I would be remiss if I did not also acknowledge the consequences that can come from compliance. We want students to follow rules, but we also want them to question rules and to stand up when they see a wrong; we want them to think for themselves. This point is discussed further in the chapter on integrity.)

The Steps to Developing Self-Control

There are five basic steps to developing self-control:

1. Developing awareness
2. Complying
3. Goal setting
4. Transferring
5. Monitoring

Step 1: Developing Awareness

Students need to become conscious of the importance of self-control before they can learn it. It's possible that many see it simply as "doing what you are told," but, of course, it's more than that. Teachers should make a point of talking about its importance and illustrate how people who have been successful—whether in school, literature, or the everyday world—have been so because they have exercised self-control in some aspect of their performance. It's best to elicit student awareness through class discussion, working from real-life examples of people whose success in life is due largely to exercising self-control. (It can be easy for students to think that people succeed, well, *just because* and not thanks to specific success skills.)

Step 2: Complying

Once students have developed an awareness of the importance of self-control, the next step is for them to attempt exercising theirs by complying with school rules and teacher directions. At the same time, educators should make students aware of why specific rules or directions are necessary and discuss with them why compliance can be difficult. Students develop self-control not just by following the rules but by being conscious and thoughtful about why they do so and what temptations they are resisting (e.g., playing with friends or a game on their computer). We want students to be thoughtful, question authority, and to stand up for what's right (see the chapter on *integrity* for more on this.)

Step 3: Goal Setting

During this step, students set one academic and one personal goal related to self-control. By setting goals for behaviors both in and out of school, students are better able to transfer self-control skills from one setting to another. When drafting each goal, students should identify three specific components: the ultimate objective, the obstacles or distractions they'll need to overcome to meet that objective (so that they are aware of the self-control that will be required), and how they will determine success. Ideally, students will draft their goals using a form such as the one in Figure 3.2 and discuss them with a teacher before considering them set. This interaction—ensuring that goals are realistic and that obstacles have been anticipated—will play a significant role in helping students succeed.

FIGURE 3.2			
Self-Control Goals			
	Ultimate Objective	**Obstacle(s) or Distraction(s)**	**Metrics for Success**
Scholastic Goal			
Personal Goal			

Examples of scholastic goals include allocating enough time to complete homework (using self-control to avoid distractions), remaining attentive in class (using self-control to resist talking to friends), being on time to class (using self-control not to linger in the halls), and so on. Personal goals could be as specific as improving as an artist (using self-control to practice diligently and routinely) or as broad as being kinder to friends or not arguing with parents (using self-control to restrain negative emotions). In all cases, the goals should be reasonable and potential obstacles or distractions should be specified. It's important, especially early on, for students to be able to meet their goals so that they can gain confidence in their ability to succeed.

Goals that aren't shared are no more than hopes, and sharing them is the first step in being held accountable for them. Of course, we need to respect every student's comfort level as he or she shares. One idea is to write the goals out on a chart hanging on the wall or displayed on the white board; kids can periodically show their progress with a checkmark ("I'm on target"), a hyphen ("I'm not sure"), or an X ("I'm in trouble"). If students prefer to share goals privately, they can do so in one-on-one conversations with the teacher or by sealing their goals in an envelope and handing it to the teacher.

We often fail to meet our goals because we lose focus (who remembers New Year's resolutions by the time May rolls around?), so it's important for students to regularly reflect on and share their progress. Students who are comfortable sharing their goals with one another can meet in teams of three or four for 10 minutes every week to share how they're doing. Teachers should make clear to them that they are sharing so that they can be held accountable for their goals and support one another in trying to meet them. Students should practice active listening and encouraging talk in their groups. (As noted earlier, too much self-control can be inhibiting and create difficulties for some students, so teachers need to be particularly aware of how this focus has an impact on each child.)

Step 4: Transferring

Once students have set their goals and had time to pursue them, it is time for them to discuss how they might transfer the lessons about self-control that they learned during this process to other situations. Teachers can help students reflect on how they were able to transcend obstacles or distractions and how they might do likewise in pursuit of different goals. One of the keys to a strong sense of self-control is drawing from experiences when new challenges arise. A teacher may ask, "How can what we learned about the role of self-control in achieving goals be used in other situations?" Over time, again reflecting the age and developmental level of children, teachers can help students reflect on how the obstacles that they have identified may be similar to those that were overcome when other goals have been met.

By reflecting on their own experiences, students might develop new goals related to self-control with varying levels of specificity. Here are some examples:

- I need to focus more on giving time to my little sister.
- I will count my calories and only eat dessert on the weekend.
- I will devote 90 minutes to my homework even if I think I have completed it before then.
- I will make a point of not sitting by my friends in math class.
- I will count to seven before I respond if I feel criticized at the dinner table.

What's most important is for students to learn how to actively exercise self-control, realize its importance, anticipate challenges, and develop strategies for staying focused on their goals.

Step 5: Monitoring

Monitoring progress on the goals and revising them when necessary helps students identify their most effective self-control strategies. It's not enough that they develop self-control in a situation and achieve their goals (although that's good!); they need to understand what they did and why it worked for them so that they can use what they learned in other situations.

Self-Control as a Habit

Intention and effort can develop self-control. Roy Baumeister, a professor at Florida State University, notes that

> engaging in some extra self-control activities for a couple weeks produces improvement in self-control, even on tasks that have no relation to the exercise activities. The exercises can be arbitrary, such as using your left hand instead of your right hand to open doors and brush your teeth. Or they can be meaningful, such as working to manage money better and save more. The important thing is to practice overriding habitual ways of doing things and exerting deliberate control over your actions. Over time, that practice improves self-control. (Weir, 2012, p. 36)

Similarly, Duhigg (2012) writes that "the best way to strengthen willpower and give students a leg up, studies indicate, is to make it into a habit" (p. 131). We do this, he says, when we choose "a certain behavior ahead of time, and then [follow] that routine when the inflection point arrives" (p. 146). He goes on to quote Angela Duckworth: "Sometimes it looks like people with great self-control aren't working hard—but that's because they've made it automatic" (p. 131).

Today, when children and adults often carry their e-distractions with them everywhere, students need to develop the habit of self-control more than ever. How many times have you seen people sitting at a restaurant table, talking while simultaneously checking their phones? How often do you see teachers and administrators checking their phones—sometimes surreptitiously, sometimes not—during faculty meetings? Increasing overprotectiveness is another challenge to self-control. Often, it seems, today's parents are most focused on protecting children from everything, including themselves, rather than on allowing them the necessary freedom to develop personal willpower in different situations.

Strategies for Developing Self-Control

For all teachers:

• **Have students set two academic goals:** an *achievement goal* reflecting the knowledge and skills students hope to acquire, and a *process goal* focused on how best to exercise self-control in pursuing the achievement goal.

• **Work to create a classroom climate in which kids support one another's efforts at gaining self-control.** Here's an example from Chris Hass, a teacher at the Center for Inquiry school in Columbia, South Carolina (personal communication, October 14, 2015):

> Whenever my students struggle with self-control, I'll sit down with them and tell them what I see and invite them to help me think of a solution. They have learned what it is to play school, so they'll often suggest punishments I could dole out. But I push them to do more than think punitively. I ask them for strategies that might help us avoid the situations in which we so often see other people, or ourselves, getting into trouble. We talk about ways each of us could be responsible not only for the collective behavior of the classroom but for each of our individual actions as well.
>
> When we see behavior as something we are all responsible for, we begin to help one another out. For instance, if someone

has trouble transitioning without becoming a significant distraction in the classroom, someone else might put a gentle hand on the student's shoulder and remind him or her to focus. If building community has been a priority up to this point and the kids have built strong trusting relationships with one another, this act will be accepted as a demonstration of caring and not an attempt at authority over peers.

• **Develop a mindfulness practice.** Chris Wallach, a teacher at New City School in St. Louis, Missouri, has done this. She routinely practices mindfulness with her students, colleagues, and students' parents. "Using the practice of mindfulness, we are able calm our bodies and minds," she says. "The simple action of focusing on our breath creates the foundation for lessons on self-awareness and self-control" (personal communication, September 27, 2015). Wallach recommends a series of videos about mindfulness designed for teenagers (http://mindfulnessforteens.com) as well as one that features celebrities discussing their mindfulness. You can see the video here: www.youtube.com/watch?time_continue=3&v=up3MZuYkf-g.

For middle or high school teachers:

• **Share some of the self-control quotes in this chapter to start discussions with students.** Ask, "Are there ways in which these quotes conflict? Do you see instances of what they are saying in your life?"

• **Lead a discussion about whether it's possible to have too much self-control (answer: it is) and how that might be problematic.**

• **Ask students to rate their levels of self-control regarding various household duties and consider why they might have more self-control with some unpleasant duties than with others.** It might be interesting to do this in the context of multiple intelligences: Do students have more or less self-control on, say, linguistic tasks than bodily-kinesthetic ones?

• **Examine literature through the lens of self-control.** What characters exercise appropriate self-control, and what characters don't? How might a plot have evolved very differently (or not at all) if certain characters had more or less self-control?

- **Discuss how self-control relates to the other Formative Five success skills (empathy, integrity, grit, and embracing diversity).** This is also a good way to reinforce the importance of the Formative Five.

- **Have students consider what kinds of jobs might require the most self-control.** Then ask them if they think the high need for self-control is a function of the job or the individual who is doing it. Does a job require more self-control because precision is required or because the distractions or temptations are greater? Could it be both?

- **Ask students to find examples from news sources of people who *uncharacteristically* failed to use self-control (e.g., a well-respected banker who is indicted for siphoning funds).** The "uncharacteristically" is important because news accounts are rife with people demonstrating a lack of self-control; the point here is to identify a situation in which it is an exception and then speculate on what might have happened.

- **Ask students to identify lyrics from popular music that proclaim the value or challenges of self-control (although the term self-control is not likely to be used).**

- **Identify political candidates whose careers were derailed due to poor self-control.** (There is, unfortunately, no shortage of examples.)

For elementary teachers:

- **Have students set personal goals for each reporting period.** These could be taken from a category on the report card or related to one of the other Formative Five success skills. "I will do a better job of sitting and listening" and "I will keep my desk organized" are both good examples. At New City School, students in grades 2–6 set two goals each year, one focused on scholastic improvement and another on one of the "personal intelligence" qualities listed on their report cards (confidence, motivation, problem solving, responsibility, effort and work habits, appreciation for diversity, and teamwork).

- **Create a system to help students monitor their self-control.** For example, students might write their goals on a notecard and tape it to their desks. Either randomly or at predesignated times, students can check on their progress and share with the teacher.

• **Help students anticipate situations where maintaining self-control might be difficult.** For example, if students have trouble exercising self-control at lunch or during recess, the teacher can ask them to think about the consequences of their actions and how they might change their ways (perhaps through brief "touch-base" meetings before these times).

• **Use "problem-solving chairs" in the classroom.** This idea comes from retired New City School teacher Carla Duncan. Students have the right to ask classmates to join them in the chairs to talk about obstacles or distractions that might be impeding their self-control. Ideally, the teacher should monitor from a distance and not get involved. The goal is to help children adequately anticipate and address challenges.

• **Facilitate a class discussion on the role of self-control in art.** Are some forms of art more dependent upon self-control? Is self-control an essential part of any creativity?

• **Facilitate a class discussion on the relationship between location and self-control.** Are there some physical spaces where people need to exhibit more self-control than in others? Are there places where self-control doesn't really matter?

For principals:

• **Build developing or improving self-control into every teacher's professional goal-setting process.** Teachers must model the self-control that they want students to develop. This should be presented in the context of teaching the Formative Five, adults developing self-control so that we can help our students do the same. Principals might ask teachers to share any obstacles or distractions that they anticipate having to surmount. Of course, principals should also serve as role models and share their self-control efforts with faculty (both successes and not-yet-there stories).

• **Remind faculty that self-control has many aspects.** Losing weight or quitting smoking are classic examples of goals requiring a lot of self-control, but willpower is just as important in any number of contexts. Kevin Dwyer, a graduate of the New City School, shared that for him, self-control "isn't just resisting the fourth donut, but it's also maintaining control over your thoughts." He cites racism as an example, noting that we all need to develop and use self-control so that we don't fall prey to stereotypes and generalizations. (I expand on this point in Chapter 5.) "We should not let our base emotions dictate our lives," he notes. "We can experience them, but we should control them" (personal communication, January 30, 2016).

- **Ask teachers to reflect on how they have developed and used self-control in their teaching.** Principals might consider sharing the following powerful example from Andrew Gallagher, a middle school teacher in the St. Louis Public Schools (shared in a personal communication on November 12, 2015):

> Just last year, for the first time in a very long time, I had a student direct some very colorful language at me so loudly and force- fully that a very large classroom of students working in groups fell dead silent. Obviously, I had no other option but to address it directly and in the moment.
>
> I would be lying if I said my adrenaline wasn't pumping—I was completely unused to language like that being directed at me, particularly from a student who had always been remark- ably amicable with me (though occasionally prickly with class- mates). I collected myself and said to her, "Let's speak outside." I didn't yell because I didn't need to—the class was as quiet as a grave. Thankfully, the student complied without arguing.
>
> I made a conscious decision before our talk to let her speak first. The situation to me called for firmness, but also forbear- ance. After about 30 seconds of silence and staring at the wall, the student broke down crying—heavy, wracking sobs. She dou- bled over and sat down. When I hugged her and helped her to collect herself, she shared with me that her cousin had been bru- tally murdered the night before.

Instead of punishing her, I made her promise me that she would help with our school's peer-mediation group. She did. And over the course of the year, she became without question the best student in my class. To this day, she visits my classroom regularly even though she's no longer my student. Had I lost my self-control after her outburst, or had I not given her a chance to put her behavior in context, our relationship would likely have ended up in a very different place.

- **Facilitate a discussion among teachers and parents of Paul Tough's article "Can the Right Kind of Play Teach Self-Control?" (2009).** The article suggests that we should think about play as framing children's future development.
- **Establish a faculty committee to look into ways to develop students' self-control** *that require no additional personnel, rules, procedures, or penalties.* In doing this, consider mindfulness as a strategy worth pursuing. An article in the *Journal of Child and Family Studies* by Rachel Razza and colleagues looked at whether mindfulness could help develop self-control and concluded that

> by the end of the school year the children who had been practicing mindfulness were less impulsive and better able to wait for a potential reward—in other words, they became more like the kids who could wait for that second treat in the Marshmallow Test. . . . What's more, the program had the strongest effect on the children whose self-regulation skills were the weakest at the beginning of the year. (Razza, Bergen-Cico, & Raymond, 2015)

Books That Support the Development of Self-Control

Picture books:

- *Mouse Was Mad* (2009), by Linda Urban
- *David Gets in Trouble* (2002), by David Shannon

- *Interrupting Chicken* (2010), by David Ezra Stein
- *Lilly's Purple Plastic Purse* (1996), by Kevin Henkes

Chapter books:

- *True . . . Sort Of* (2011), by Katherine Hannigan
- *Takedown* (2006), by Rich Wallace

4

Integrity

Dark times lie ahead of us and there will be a time when we must choose between what is easy and what is right.

—Albus Dumbledore in *Harry Potter and the Goblet of Fire*

Chloe could always be counted upon to tell the truth. She took responsibility for her behavior and would mention when her academic efforts or personal conduct fell short of her own expectations. In this regard, she was her own worst critic. In fact, she was so forthright that I was careful not to ask her questions in public, lest her candidness alienate her peers. Though she was very popular, Chloe didn't hesitate to tell her friends when she thought they were acting inappropriately. But her integrity didn't always come easily—it was clear that she worked to be an honest and responsible person.

Lander was never in trouble but was always on the periphery of a problem. If there was a disruption in class, one of Lander's friends was likely to be pegged as the initiator while Lander was off in the shadows. By watching his eye contact with classmates whenever trouble was afoot, it became clear to me over time that Lander was often manipulating the action from offstage. On those moments when other students called out Lander as the instigator, he was always able to manage a credible excuse—and, later, would ensure that the kids who identified him were ostracized from his clique. Substitute teachers liked Lander because he came across as a helpful do-gooder; they weren't around him long enough to appreciate that he was actually a talented manipulator. Because of his cleverness, Lander maintained a decent academic record that obscured his penchant for duplicity.

We've all enjoyed dealing with Chloes, and we've all been worried about Landers. As educators, we need to teach students like Lander to exhibit greater integrity. If we don't, I worry not only about him and his life's prospects but also about the people close to him. Just as someone exhibiting integrity elevates the behaviors of others, so too can a lack of it have deleterious effects on individuals and groups.

Figure 4.1 shows the self-assessment survey for *integrity*. Take a moment to answer the questions before continuing with this chapter.

What Is Integrity?

Integrity stems from honesty, but is a higher, more public form of action. *Merriam-Webster* defines honesty as "fairness and straightforwardness of conduct; adherence to the facts" and integrity as "firm adherence to a code of especially moral or artistic values; incorruptibility." It is possible to be honest without displaying integrity, but it is not possible to have integrity without honesty.

Though it would be a Sisyphean task to try to rank the relative value of the Formative Five success skills, integrity is the one most often mentioned as essential by employers. Certainly that's the attitude of Warren Buffett, the multibillionaire and CEO of Berkshire Hathaway: "In looking for people to hire, you look for three qualities: integrity, intelligence, and energy. And if they don't have the first, the other two will kill you." In fact, integrity is crucial to every sector of society. As Bob Marley once put it, "The greatness of a man is not in how much wealth he acquires, but in his integrity and his ability to affect those around him positively."

FIGURE 4.1

Self-Assessment Survey: Integrity

Note: The following survey is designed to provide a sense of your feelings about integrity. It is a tool to elicit reflection and discussion, not a scientifically valid instrument.

Directions: Place a 1 (strongly disagree), 2 (disagree), 3 (not sure), 4 (agree), or 5 (strongly agree) after each item.

1. I look for opportunities to highlight honest behaviors among both my students and the literary and historical figures that we study. ___
2. Students need to know that decisions about honesty are not limited to financial matters. ___
3. If people are unfair or dishonest with you, it's appropriate to act that way with them. ___
4. Honesty and integrity are attributes best learned outside of school. ___
5. There are times when I should speak out about an injustice but I find myself reluctant to do so. ___
6. I try to be a role model and let my students know how I react in situations that call for honesty and integrity. ___
7. A zero-tolerance policy helps to instill integrity in students because most situations are black and white. ___
8. Honesty is always subjective. ___
9. Public displays of integrity can be harder than simply being honest. ___
10. Leadership requires more than quiet honesty. ___

Scoring:

___ (A) Total points for 1, 2, 6, 9, 10

___ (B) Total points for 3, 4, 5, 7, 8

___ (C) Subtract (B) from (A) for your "teaching for integrity" score

If you scored

- *18 or higher:* You fully understand the issue of integrity!
- *15–17:* You understand integrity but may need to work more directly on it with your students.
- *12–14:* You should probably focus more on integrity in your classroom instruction.
- *11 or lower:* You would probably benefit from reading up on or joining a discussion group about integrity.

Note: You can find an integrity self-assessment survey for students in Appendix A.

George Peternel, the retired associate director of the Northwestern University Center for Talent Development, noted that he'd "never met a person whom [he] respected who did not exhibit a high level of integrity," and "that few, if any, people can succeed for any length of time in any workplace without the respect of colleagues, subordinates and superordinates. Not to mention in the world outside of work where all relationships, including and especially marriages, where integrity sustains and nurtures the relationship" (personal communication, January 26, 2016). Likewise, First Lady Michelle Obama highlighted the importance of integrity when she said, "We learned about honesty and integrity—that the truth matters . . . that you don't take shortcuts or play by your own set of rules . . . and success doesn't count unless you earn it fair and square" (Cassidy, 2012).

First, Be Honest

Of all of the Formative Five success skills, educators are likely to think of integrity as the one we do the best job teaching. We start early: kindergartners learn about George Washington purportedly proclaiming, "I cannot tell a lie." Honesty is esteemed and promoted in every classroom, and that's as it should be. Although educators and parents can disagree about a lot, they speak the same voice when it comes to valuing honesty. Teachers and principals indeed do a good job of focusing on honesty—but we need to pay more attention to integrity.

Being honest is a response—to a comment, a question, a situation, or an opportunity. We may be alone or in a group, acting privately or in public. It is also rooted in choice: we can respond honestly or not. Some examples of when students face this choice:

- The teacher stops writing on the board and turns to the giggling class. "Who made that noise?" he asks.
- The principal asks a group of students who were sent to her office, "OK now, who started this fight?"

- "Frederick," the teacher says, "the writing in the report you submitted doesn't sound like you. Is there something you want to tell me?
- Bobby catches a glance of a studious classmate's test and sees that she has circled (B) in response to a question where he circled (A).
- It's late, the assignment is due tomorrow morning, and Sally has only now begun to do research for her report. She discovers an online source that has all the information she needs—and that sounds like something she could have written.

Of course, we confront decisions about honesty all the time as adults:

- You've accepted a dinner invitation to join a small group of friends, but then a second invite arrives from someone you'd rather be with for the same evening.
- The salesperson mistakenly undercharged you for the shirt you purchased, but you only notice when you look at your receipt after the sale is completed.
- The tax form asks you to indicate how many deductions you are claiming for the previous year.
- You're about to mail a birthday card, so you go to the school office to buy stamps—and notice that the postage machine is activated and no one is around.

Sometimes, making an honest decision requires us to think a matter through; other times, it occurs instantaneously, without us being aware that we're making a decision. For some people, doing the right thing is deeply ingrained—and that's how we'd like it to be for our students (and ourselves). To that end, teachers must teach honesty directly. It's important for students to realize that we can exhibit more or less honesty depending on the situation, and that it can often be harder to maintain it in private than in public. Asking, "What effect does what your friends think have on how you might behave?" is a good way to open up student reflection on the subject. The more realistic and relevant our lessons and discussions are, the more likely it is that students will understand and internalize them.

The need to manifest honesty is all the more important in our current era of social media. Our ability to communicate instantaneously over the internet has opened up the world, exponentially increasing the number and types of the people with whom we interact—but it can also work against us building deeper, more trusting relationships. One look at online comments sections in newspapers will confirm that electronic communication makes it much easier for people to be dishonest and act in uncivil ways. I have noticed that when commenters are allowed to contribute anonymously, nastier opinions tend to appear. People can hide behind their screen names and act in ways that they never would dare to if they were being held accountable. Further, this lack of honesty and care isn't limited to anonymous comments on blogs. How often do we read an e-mail that causes us to raise our eyebrows because it sounds so unlike the sender we know? Communicating through the internet reduces the personal connection, and it's easier for honesty to be lost. The fact that today so many of our interactions are electronic means that being confident about others' trust and integrity is even more important today than in it has been in the past.

Moving from Honesty to Integrity

Whereas honesty can be private and innate, integrity is always public and developed intentionally—when we act with integrity, we are consciously making our personal values known to others. Writing on the Alliance for Integrity website, Jim Thomas notes, "The major difference between honesty and integrity is that one may be entirely honest without engaging in the thought and reflection integrity demands" (2011). Integrity means being responsible for our actions and owning our roles in solving problems. And because it is *interpersonal* in nature (unlike honesty, which is *intrapersonal*), it is a key component in becoming a successful leader. By teaching and promoting integrity, we help our students become leaders and change agents who feel a commitment to take a stand and make things right.

It is possible—and actually pretty common—for people to have honesty without integrity. Consider the example of a student named Linda. She is always truthful, keeps her word, and wouldn't think of keeping the money if an error were made in her favor. But Linda also fails to intervene if a friend is dishonest or benefits unfairly from a mistake. If she sees another student cheating, she turns her head. Linda lacks integrity. She is honest, but feels no obligation to be true to her values and step up when the occasion demands it.

To be clear, we absolutely should be exhorting and developing honesty in our students, but we should not stop there. Integrity is being accountable for what we do by acknowledging our responsibility and stepping forward to own our role in finding a solution to the problem. Integrity carries our value of honesty to a higher level. By teaching and promoting integrity, we help our students become leaders and change agents, people who feel a commitment to take a stand and make things right.

There are five steps to progressing from honesty to integrity:

1. Becoming aware of what honesty means
2. Internalizing and acting with honesty
3. Becoming aware of what integrity means
4. Identifying opportunities for integrity
5. Initiating situations to manifest integrity

This developmental sequence of honesty evolving to integrity is depicted in Figure 4.2. (Note: The chart implies more of a linear sequence than is reality. When learning a complex skill or attitude, progress is never smooth or always consistent.) Another way to view the continuum of honesty to integrity is shown in Figure 4.3.

In his book *Integrity*, Stephen Carter says that it "demands a difficult process of discerning one's deepest understanding of right and wrong, and then further requires action consistent with what one has learned. It is possible to be honest without ever taking a hard look inside one's soul, to say nothing of taking any action based on what one finds" (1996, p. 10).

FIGURE 4.2
The Steps of Teaching Honesty and Integrity

Honesty to Integrity Developmental Levels	Honesty to Integrity Actions
1. Aware of *honesty* as a general personal, human, and community good	Identifies honest versus dishonest behavior from questions or prompts
2. Internalizes *honesty* as a quality that should be embodied and acts honestly	Acts honestly regardless of whether others are aware of the behavior
3. Aware of what *integrity* means and how it differs from and goes beyond *honesty*	Identifies if an individual is showing honesty or integrity
4. Identifies interactions and situations in which *integrity* could be manifested	Seeks and creates opportunities to show integrity
5. Accepts the need to show *integrity* in pursuing what is right, even if it is costly	Manifests integrity in interactions and situations

Of course, taking action is not always easy, even if you're fully confident that your position is correct. According to Brené Brown, "integrity is choosing courage over comfort; choosing what is right over what is fun, fast, or easy; and choosing to practice our values rather than simply professing them" (2015, p. 123).

In almost any situation, the honest response is fairly obvious —the difficulty lies in choosing it over the dishonest response. Integrity is much more of a challenge to teach, especially when exhibiting integrity might

FIGURE 4.3
Honesty and Integrity

Behavior	Honesty	Integrity
Discerning	X	
Acting/Responding	X	
Saying openly		X
Initiating/Creating		X

well mean refusing to comply with classroom or school rules and regulations. As Carter points out, "many of the most honored figures in the pantheon of integral Americans are people we admire precisely because of their willingness to break laws they considered unjust" (1996, p. 180).

Trust me, I understand that students *do* need to comply with rules—in my 37 years leading schools, I spent a lot more time dealing with rule breakers than I would have liked. Too often, I would return from supervising the lunchroom to find the bench outside the main office full of students who'd been sent to see me for noncompliance. (To be fair, although they never sat on the bench, it was sometimes the *adults* in the building who had the most difficulty following rules!) Adherence to rules is necessary for an organization to function effectively, but it is naïve to expect that our students can develop integrity without ever questioning them. (I've been to a school where students are expected not only to stand in line quietly in the hall but to ensure that their feet are aligned with the floor tiles so that the lines they form are perfectly straight. While I can appreciate the need for clear expectations and order, I can't help but wonder what students are losing by having to follow this kind of protocol.)

Challenges of Teaching Integrity

Of course, teaching integrity gets quite complicated because what is perceived as fair and just by one person can often be considered unfair and unjust by another. Today, a majority of Americans would view the actions of Dr. Martin Luther King Jr. as just, but that wasn't the case when he was visibly displaying his integrity by working as a civil rights activist. Similarly, today there are protests against police shootings of unarmed black males as well as counter-protests in favor of the police, and protests both for and against legal abortion. These issues confound and frustrate adults, let alone children, so they make teaching integrity a challenge—but a necessary one.

One teacher at my school purposely orchestrated unjust situations for students (e.g., taxing students for the paper they use or their trips to the restroom) after teaching them about the Boston Tea Party. Invariably, the students would protest her unfair actions. Even though they knew it was a class activity, they felt the injustice and need to respond. This is an effective way to help students understand the meaning of integrity—both their responsibility to exhibit it and its potential to right injustices. As Carter says, "the rest of what we think matters very little if we lack essential integrity, the courage of our convictions" (1996, p. 7).

In teaching both honesty and integrity, we need to consciously articulate the trade-offs and rationales behind our thinking. An honest act becomes one of integrity when we share it with others—and by sharing examples of our own integrity with students, we can serve as role models for them.

Strategies for Developing Integrity

For all teachers:

• **Model honesty by quickly and visibly admitting to mistakes.** When kids see adults do this, they receive a powerful message.

• **Model integrity by talking about values and intervening in unfair situations.** There is much to be gained by being transparent and explaining your rationale to students.

• **Help students understand that there are often difficult consequences for acting with integrity.** That doesn't mean we shy away from doing this; rather, it means that we are aware and we anticipate how we will respond when particular kinds of situations arise.

• **Make a point of routinely applauding students when they step up to do the right thing.** Sometimes we need to deliberately work to reinforce qualities that don't receive grades.

• **Use the "Values Card Sort" exercise to help students think about what matters to them.** Students receive 80-plus cards, featuring terms (e.g., *acceptance, accuracy, beauty, caring, courtesy*) and brief definitions for each. They are then asked to sort the cards into three categories: "Not important to me," "Important to me," and "Very important to me." Ginny Fendell of Whitfield School in St. Louis, Missouri, uses this exercise to develop integrity by helping students understand their personal values. After sorting their cards, students can discuss why they made their decisions and can compare their sorts. Another option is to have students sort the cards in a group to highlight their different values and perspectives. Older students might examine whether there appears to be any correlation between where the cards are placed and the gender or race of the student.

(A detailed explanation of the activity can be found at www.thegood project.org/toolkits-curricula/the-goodwork-toolkit/value-sort-activity/ and the actual Value Sort cards can be seen here: http://casaa.unm.edu /inst/Personal%20Values%20Card%20Sort.pdf. Created by Miller, Baca, Matthews, and Wilbourne, this instrument is in the public domain.)

Extend the Values Card Sort activity by then having students work in a group to try to determine where a card should be placed. This can be difficult, and it highlights the different perspectives and values that people hold. Doing this, a teacher should be prepared to conclude the exercise by asking students to identify patterns and themes of agreement and commonality (rather than letting the class end with everyone focusing on how people differ).

For middle or high school teachers:

• **Help students understand the difference between honesty and integrity.** Teachers might post definitions of the two words in their classrooms and remind students that we cannot settle simply for being honest—we should strive to display integrity as well. Teachers should ask students how particular situations might have evolved differently if the people involved had exhibited more integrity.

• **Ask students to find instances of honesty and integrity in the news.** If students identify individuals as behaving honestly, teachers should first applaud the individuals' honesty and then ask students what the individual(s) might have additionally done to also demonstrate integrity.

• **Raise the issue of peer influence on questions of honesty and integrity by asking students if they act more or less honest in different situations—and why.**

- **Use the tale of the ring of Gyges from Plato's *Republic* to help students understand integrity.** Mark Norwood, currently a teacher at Crossroads College Preparatory School in St. Louis, says he did this when he taught 6th graders at New City School. "I told them only the beginning of the story at first, where the ring is turned around and the wearer becomes invisible but can still see and hear all that is going on," he said (personal communication, December 6, 2015). He would then have his students write about and discuss what they would do if they had the option of becoming invisible. (Going to the movies without paying was one answer.)

"The real learning came when we discussed why Plato wrote the story," he continued, "which centers on the question of whether something is wrong in and of itself or only because we're afraid to get caught. Our 6th graders were left thinking about integrity and the importance of being consistent when it comes to what they believe is right and wrong."

- **Facilitate a discussion on whether or not integrity changes over time or is affected by context.** From historical changes in voter eligibility to slavery to the role of religious institutions in times of war, countless topics lend themselves to such a discussion. Ronald H. Balson's historical novel *Once We Were Brothers* (2010) vividly raises the issue of integrity in Nazi Germany, as does Erik Larson's *In the Garden of Beasts* (2011). Another good resource is T. C. Boyle's *The Tortilla Curtain* (1995), which examines the lives of undocumented immigrants in the United States and the role that integrity plays in their lives.

For elementary teachers:

- **Talk with students about the relationship between responsibility and honesty.** An important aspect of honesty is taking responsibility for your actions and admitting mistakes even when they're not obvious to anyone else.
- **With input from students, create a compact that sets out expectations for student behaviors.** At my school, for example, 2nd- and 3rd-grade teachers took time early in the year to discuss appropriate restroom behavior with students, eliciting their ideas, creating an

agreement, having everyone sign it, and posting it on the restroom walls. The hope was that seeing their signatures on the poster every time they entered the restroom would have a positive effect on students' behavior.

• **Have students identify characters from literature who are honest, along with those who do and do not display very strong integrity.**

• **Routinely ask students how they would respond in specific situations that warrant honesty and integrity.** As the semester evolves, teachers should present students with increasingly complicated and ambiguous situations. It's a good idea to have students ponder their answers for about 30 seconds and then discuss them in groups of four or five. This exercise has the benefit of exposing students to other people's thinking processes and problem-solving strategies, and it encourages them to publicly state their opinions (thus demonstrating integrity).

• **Ask students to list ways in which they might display honesty and integrity at home, at school, and at recess, listing three for each category.** Teachers can collect students' lists and share them with the whole class before having them break into small groups for discussion. Children often understand the role of integrity in situations involving cheating or money (e.g., they know not to take loose change without asking), but can fail to see its role in other types of contexts (e.g., admitting that they don't know something rather than fabricating an answer).

• **Help children begin to anticipate and internalize integrity by teaching them to follow "The Grandma Rule" by asking, "How would you feel if your grandma knew you were doing this?"** (This strategy was shared with me by Mark Norwood, noted earlier.)

For principals:

• **Educate faculty about the difference between honesty and integrity.** Focusing on integrity doesn't mean taking honesty for granted, but rather moving beyond it and preparing students to take leadership roles in schools.

• **Model integrity at faculty meetings and student assemblies by sharing personal stories of times when you did the right thing despite facing adversity.** Too often, these types of decisions aren't readily visible to others. This can be hard to do because we don't want to appear to be bragging or setting ourselves up as perfect people, but just as with teachers and students, there is power in the leader sharing her decisions—actions and rationale—when faced with a situation where integrity was needed.

- **Consciously work to establish a norm of trust.** This means both talking about trust with students and also giving them enough leeway to respond to situations in ways that earn the trust. Craig Hinkle, a principal in the Dallas Independent School District, says, "It's amazing how students respond to real trust—and it is imperative that they learn this success skill as they become adults responsible for our mortgages, bank accounts, prescriptions, and even for us as neighbors when tornadoes and floods rearrange our lives" (personal communication, January 26, 2016).

- **Use the Values Card Sort exercise discussed earlier at a faculty meeting.** This not only facilitates faculty members' reflections about their integrity, it makes it more likely that they will do this activity with their students.

I hope that all of the ideas and strategies to advance integrity presented here can be helpful to teachers. At the same time, I understand that there exist systemic reasons why teaching integrity can be difficult in schools. Jarin Jaffee, head of Evansville Day School in Evansville, Indiana, makes the point well:

> I would argue that to a large extent kids inherently possess integrity and it is the conditions of school (namely standardized testing and an obsession regarding grades) and life thereafter that erode this natural attribute. I think a similar argument can be made with creativity (the Marshmallow Challenge is a prime example). So for integrity, cultivating a school and classroom culture that promotes collaboration and rewards teamwork is one avenue, as is trusting students to develop and lead an honor system that puts kids at the foundation of school culture. (personal communication, October 26, 2015)

Books That Support the Development of Integrity

Picture books:

- *Amazing Grace* (1991), by Mary Hoffman and Caroline Binch
- *Mr. Peabody's Apples* (2003), by Madonna
- *Jamaica and the Substitute Teacher* (1999), by Juanita Havill
- *Honest to Goodness Truth* (2000), by Patricia McKissack

Chapter books:

- *The Jacket* (2001), by Andrew Clements
- *Junie B. Jones Is Not a Crook* (1997), by Barbara Park

5

Embracing Diversity

Diversity is about all of us, and about us having to figure out how to walk through this world together.

—Jacqueline Woodson, author

René is a member of her school's Gay-Straight Alliance and spends a few hours each week volunteering to teach low-income students how to read. She deliberately seeks experiences with people from other cultures and friendships with people of other hues. It's clear that she accepts and appreciates others who are different than she is. René has held many leadership positions in student government because she has befriended so many students, representing a range of different identities and groups.

Lana sticks to her "own kind," as she would phrase it, with a sense of awareness and pride. She is uncomfortable with others who are not of her race or socioeconomic status. Lana leads a very tight and homogenous clique. She tends to ridicule those who are different than she is and exhibits a sense of superiority toward just about everybody. Her band of friends is as narrow as her taste in music. She shows little curiosity about other countries and cultures.

Figure 5.1 shows the self-assessment survey for *embracing diversity*. Take a moment to answer the questions before continuing with this chapter.

FIGURE 5.1

Self-Assessment Survey: Embracing Diversity

Note: The following survey is designed to provide a sense of your feelings about embracing diversity. It is a tool to elicit reflection and discussion, not a scientifically valid instrument.

Directions: Place a 1 (strongly disagree), 2 (disagree), 3 (not sure), 4 (agree), or 5 (strongly agree) after each item.

1. I am comfortable discussing diversity with students and colleagues. ___
2. My personal identity plays no role in how I teach. ___
3. The signs and decorations in my classroom reflect various cultures and races. ___
4. How likely students think they are to succeed has a lot of bearing on their success. ___
5. Students' backgrounds are not relevant once they enter my class. ___
6. By focusing solely on my curriculum's scope and sequence, I give every child an equal chance to succeed. ___
7. I regularly seek opportunities to highlight contributions to society from people of races or ethnicities that are underrepresented at my school. ___
8. Diversity considerations should focus only on race and ethnicity. ___
9. My students are comfortable reporting harassment or discriminatory comments. ___
10. The curriculum, materials, and textbooks that I use are free of bias. ___

Scoring:

___ (A) Total points for 1, 3, 4, 7, 9
___ (B) Total points for 2, 5, 6, 8, 10
___ (C) Subtract (B) from (A) for your "embracing diversity" score

If you scored

- *18 or higher:* You fully understand the issue of embracing diversity!
- *15–17:* You understand embracing diversity but may need to work more directly on it with your students.
- *12–14:* You should probably focus more on embracing diversity in your classroom instruction.
- *11 or lower:* You would probably benefit from reading up on or joining a discussion group about diversity.

Note: You can find an embracing diversity self-assessment survey for students in Appendix A.

What Is Embracing Diversity?

Embracing diversity means understanding that we should recognize and appreciate the differences among us. This attitude acknowledges our history of differences while empowering every person to succeed and enables all of us to come together in a caring, respectful, and productive way.

As I note in the Introduction, *embracing diversity* is the only one of the Formative Five success skills that includes a verb. This is because I believe we need to be particularly enthusiastic about accepting the legitimacy of this skill because it too often elicits discomfort or even opposition. After all, who could be against empathy, self-control, integrity, or grit? These qualities are universally esteemed, and we all know that our students will be better prepared for the real world if they possess them. Diversity is not as universally—well, *embraced*; we may appreciate many people, but we tend to embrace only those who are close to us.

I strongly believe that we need to embrace diversity enthusiastically, particularly in a country like the United States, which has a long history of discrimination at odds with our values of freedom and tolerance. Consider that 12 U.S. presidents owned slaves at one time in their lives. Even today, though we've made remarkable progress toward a society where children and adults are judged by the content of their character rather than their skin, more progress is needed.

Anna Holmes (2015) channels the hesitation and discomfort that many feel about the term *diversity* when she asks, "How does a word become so muddled that it loses much of its meaning? How does it go from communicating something idealistic to something cynical and suspect? If that word is 'diversity,' the answer is: through a combination of overuse, imprecision, inertia, and self-serving intentions" (p. 21). She further notes that the word "has become both euphemism and cliché, convenient shorthand that gestures at inclusivity and representation without taking them seriously" (p. 22). It's because of the reactions Holmes points to that we must include *embracing* in our term for this critical skill.

Dictionary.com defines *embrace* as "to take or clasp in the arms; press to the bosom; hug" and "to take or receive gladly or eagerly; accept willingly." Embrace conveys that tolerance or acceptance of those who are different than we are is necessary, but not sufficient; beyond accepting, we must learn to value, appreciate, and hold close others who are different than we are. The phrase *embracing diversity* makes this clear.

It's particularly important for us as educators to be clear about our values—what we believe and why it is important. This is especially true for values that not everyone might hold. The New City School in St. Louis, Missouri, where I served as principal for many years, proclaims diversity as one of its four bedrock principles (the others are academics, personal intelligences, and joyful learning). We promote these principles on our website (www.newcityschool.org) and at virtually every parent and faculty meeting. In my weekly e-letter to parents, I often cite examples of how we were pursuing these principles. Diversity, I point out, is one of the key values upon which our school was based.

But even at New City School, an institution known for its commitment to these principles, the word *diversity* alone isn't sufficient. Consequently, we regularly use the phrase *diversity beyond the numbers* to convey the fact that mere numbers can't reflect all of what is important or determines success. The fact that 42 percent of our students are of color, for example, is certainly important and helpful in our pursuit of diversity, understanding, and acceptance, but that number is just a beginning. What matters most is what happens each day when our students come to school. This attitude speaks to the way that embracing diversity— understanding and appreciating others—is embedded throughout our curriculum. Adding *beyond the numbers* to *diversity* conveys our school's values and expectations the same way *embracing* does in the context of success skills. At my school we appreciate a diversity of diversities— racial, ethnic, socioeconomic, religious, age, sexual orientation, ability, and political. Our use of multiple intelligences theory in designing curriculum adds even more diversity.

The viewpoint that numbers are not sufficient and we should embrace diversity leads us to look beyond our students and work to increase the diversity awareness and comfort of all adults in our community. Several distinct parent affinity groups meet regularly to talk about diversity issues (including parents of adopted children, parents from families of color, and GLBT parents). Because we at the New City School believe strongly in facilitating dialogue about diversity and bringing people together, we held a community forum in response to the killing of Michael Brown in Ferguson, Missouri, and subsequent community protests and disruptions. (You can read an account of our Ferguson Forum in my March 2015 *Educational Leadership* column, available here: www .ascd.org/publications/educational-leadership/mar15/vol72/num06 /Responding-to-Ferguson.aspx.)

Diversity and Our Origins

Historically, the human experience has been one of focusing on how *others*—regardless of how *others* are defined—are different than we are. This is a vestige from prehistory, when many of our ancestors lived in jungles, forests, or caves, and survival depended on their vigilance and ability to quickly discern differences (what Gardner terms the "naturalist intelligence"). Given the lack of societal regulations or laws, people who didn't dress like us or share our traditions were automatically suspect— and at the time, this was appropriate! Referring to life in the Pleistocene era over 11,000 years ago, Boehm (2012) notes that "it's likely that foragers of one language or diversity group would have been prone to aggressively push aside foragers of another" (p. 77). As Goleman (2006) says, "Evolutionary theory holds that our ability to sense when we should be suspicious has been every bit as essential for human survival as our capacity for trust and cooperation" (p. 22). Simply put, recognizing and being alert to differences among people was once a vital survival skill.

Today, even though most of us are long past guarding ourselves from hungry strangers or warring tribes, we sometimes continue to harbor suspicions or buy into negative stereotypes about people because they don't look or act like us. The instinct to immediately notice our differences and judge them negatively is quick and simple, but a barrier to understanding and collaboration. "Stereotypes are a real timesaver," says Stanley McChrystal, quoting from the satirical website *The Onion*, in his book, *Team of Teams* (2015, p. 239).

Says Boehm,

> One of the remarkable things about xenophobic tendencies in contemporary hunter-gatherers, and for that matter in all humans, is that our moral codes apply fully only to within the group, be it a language group, a non-literate population that shares the same piece of real estate or the same ethnic identity, or a nation. There seems to be a special, pejorative moral 'discount' applied to cultural strangers—who are often not even considered to be fully human and therefore may be killed with little compunction. (2012, p. 135)

Diversity Today

The racism integral to the founding and development of the United States—as I mention earlier, 12 U.S. presidents owned black slaves—remains alive today. It has vitiated and conditions have improved, but it would be naïve to think that our historical struggles are no longer with us. As Coates (2015) says of black Americans, "Never forget that we were enslaved in this country longer than we have been free. Never forget that for 250 years black people were born into chains—whole generations followed by more generations who knew nothing but chains" (p. 70). Likewise, Steele (2010) points out that when it comes to race and gender—indeed, to every variable that yields stereotypes—we are all prisoners of our history: "Our social identities can strongly affect things as important as our performances in the classroom and on standardized tests, our memory capacity, our athletic performance, the pressure we feel to improve ourselves, even the comfort we have with people of different groups—all things we typically think of as being determined by individual talents, motivations, and preferences" (p. 4).

Sadly, despite our progress, it sometimes feels as though racism is more evident in the United States today than in the recent past.

According to a CNN and Kaiser Family Foundation poll in 2015, "Almost two-thirds of the public (64%) say racial tensions have increased in the country over the past decade. This includes majorities of Blacks, Hispanics, and Whites alike."

Another survey, by Teaching Tolerance, the National Education Association, and the Civil Rights Project, found that "the vast majority of teachers say their schools are free of racial and ethnic tensions" despite the fact that "federal reports show that one in four students is victimized in racial or ethnic incidents in the course of a typical school year" (Southern Poverty Law Center, 2016). And the victims aren't all students of color: "Nearly 70 percent of girls say they've been sexually harassed, 75 percent of gay students report hearing anti-gay slurs at school, and more than a third of gay students say they've been physically harassed." You can read more about this, including a school climate questionnaire, at www.tolerance.org/map-it-out.

We must recognize that teaching children to embrace diversity will be an uphill struggle because we are running counter to centuries of prejudice; we aren't starting from zero. This means both embedding diversity in lessons and creating new experiences that highlight diversity. Embedding diversity into the existing curriculum means looking for opportunities to include and highlight people who reflect a range of differences—by choosing literature that features a diversity of diversities, for example, and ensuring diverse representation at assemblies, in the art on the walls, and in guest speakers. (And of course, discussions of diversity and a diversity of representation should not be limited to Black History Month—or, for that matter, to black people.)

To highlight diversity, New City School once held a "Who's What?" assembly. We invited five adults from the community, all of whom were sitting on the stage as the students entered the auditorium. They included a white male, two white females, one black female, and one black male. Our moderator, a teacher who also served as our director of diversity, read occupational characteristics about the five people without identifying who played what role. The roles they held were a nurse, a firefighter, an accountant, a salesperson, and a university professor.

When she was done, we asked our students raise their hands and vote on who they thought played what role. Of course, we had intentionally invited adults who did not conform to traditional roles. Disappointingly—but not surprisingly—many of our kids fell into the stereotype trap, deeming that the white female was the nurse and the fireperson was a male. In fact, the nurse was a white male and the firefighter was the black female. After the voting, our guests talked a bit about their careers, all of them emphasizing the importance of doing well in school. Then our director of diversity discussed stereotypes and how we have to work against falling prey to them. Our teachers were prepared for the assembly (it had been suggested by our faculty's Diversity Committee), so they were ready to reinforce what was learned afterwards in their classrooms.

Both our history and our current conditions mean that it's not enough to teach students to understand that a diversity of diversities exists. Our world is becoming more diverse by the day, and those who succeed in life will be those who appreciate and embrace the differences among us, creating a base for understanding and trust. Working with others who are different will not be an option, but rather the norm. Increasingly, we will be collaborating with others who live in foreign countries or on distant continents and who represent different races, ethnicities, and cultures. And the United States itself is becoming more diverse: as the *New York Times* notes, "According to Pew projections, based on current trends, by 2025, no ethnic or racial group will be a majority of the population" (Preston, 2015). Indeed, according to current projections, by 2050 the largest racial group in the country will be Asian.

Barbara Thomson, author of *Words Can Hurt You* (1993) and the first director of diversity at New City School, notes that "if we fail to appreciate the diversities among us, we will fail as a nation to use ALL our human resources and that failure makes us less than our best as individuals and as a country at a time in history when surely we need 'all hands on deck' to deal with the challenges ahead" (personal communication, October 1, 2015). To once more quote Steele (1999), "you have to learn from people who part of yourself tells you are difficult to trust."

It's important to appreciate the many different types of diversity: race, religion, gender, ethnicity, sexual orientation, age, income, ability—all of these factors contribute to our personal identities, framing our perceptions both of ourselves and of others. We see the world and others differently because of who we are, and others see us through our identity. And these perceptions are reciprocal: how we see and interact with others affects how they see and interact with us, and vice versa.

The Stereotype Threat

Examples of how these perceptions affect us are captured in *Whistling Vivaldi and Other Clues to How Stereotypes Affect Us* (2010) by Claude Steele. He uses research to present how diminished performance occurs when individuals are anxious that they will be judged according to a stereotype. Researchers found that individuals' performance on tests suffered when they were reminded that according to their stereotype, they were not expected to perform well on tests. In experiments, students of color who were asked to identify their race underperformed on standardized intelligence tests, and women underperformed on mathematics tests when reminded that men typically score higher on such tests. These results speak to the power of stereotypes and self-expectations.

In our schools (and in life), students' perceptions of the ways that others see them become a reality for them, which, in turn, influences how they are seen by others—and the cycle continues. To negate stereotype threats, we must confront how we see ourselves and how others see us. (A similar but converse effect is "stereotype promise." This is when the test taker is reminded that the group in which she is a member typically does better than the norm on a test. Living up to the expectation results in increased performance in this case.)

Identity Masks

At my school, Stephanie Teachout, our director of diversity, helps educate students about stereotypes by having them create identity masks.

The students use transparent paper to make a simple mask (e.g., with holes for mouth and eyes) and construction paper to create symbols depicting their personal identities. They use different shapes and colors to represent age, race, gender, ethnicity, religion, ability, and so on. Although the shape and color of the symbols should be consistent, they should vary in size and where they're placed on each mask to indicate their relative significance to each student. Students are then asked to talk to one another wearing their masks, visibly demonstrating that our identities are filters through which all communication must pass. The symbols distract both the speaker and the person listening, and often they frame the discussion. Sometimes the size and location of a symbol are so prominent that it actually gets in the way of communication. Occasionally, the symbol isn't relevant to the discussion, though both parties can still see it. Afterward, the teacher leads the students in a discussion of how the masks influenced what they said and how this happens in real life, even without actual symbols on our cheeks or foreheads. Through this valid, experiential activity, students begin to understand how their identities affect how they see others and how they are seen.

There are many permutations to this activity. Older students might create several masks, showing the differences in how they view their identities now versus when they were younger. Was their socioeconomic status less important in elementary school? Has gender always been the major theme through which they self-identified? Perhaps they make several masks to indicate how they and others perceive these aspects of their identities in different social or geographic situations today. Or they can create different masks to indicate how they see others who are similar to and different than themselves. In the latter activity, students usually notice that the symbols masks have in common with others become much smaller (i.e., less significant) than the others.

Diversity and Perspective

Although identity is typically thought to be person-centric (a reflection of who we are) or perhaps group-centric (a reflection of a group to which we belong), we need to remember that not all of our perspectives stem from who we are today. Our history and individual experiences also affect how we see things, just as do our roles in a community or an organization.

Our occupations can contribute significantly to our identities as well. For my doctoral dissertation, for example, I studied the role-based perspectives held by many employees in a huge school system (the St. Louis Public Schools) as a court-mandated metropolitan area desegregation plan was being created. Not surprisingly, teachers, principals, and central office administrators looked at educational issues quite differently due to the roles that they played in their schools and in the organization. This was a good illustration of the fact that in addition to personal demographics and group membership, people's perspectives are also shaped by the positions they occupy.

The Importance of Emphasizing Rather Than Deemphasizing Diversity

Sometimes, often with good motives, we want to deemphasize or ignore our differences. Personally, I believe that it's neither realistic nor healthy to assume that the differences among us aren't noticed. Saying "I don't see race" to those who live and feel the effects of their skin color every single day is tantamount to, in effect, erasing them by denying their identity. It is disingenuous and dishonest to ourselves and to others. Even if race doesn't alter our behaviors toward others, it is impossible that we don't notice it. Better to say, "I see race, but that doesn't mean I judge people or treat them differently." Better yet: "I see race and I have my biases, but I try to be aware of them and not let them factor into my actions or decisions." This perspective reflects the embracing of diversity that we seek. It conveys maturity, intrapersonal intelligence, candor, and a desire to treat everyone fairly. That is a good goal for our students—and for ourselves. Ignoring or discounting aspects of our diversity can be offensive, counterproductive, and even illegal. What's important is that we help one another become aware of the biases and perspectives that we have and that are all around us so that we can see one another clearly and work well together regardless of our differences.

Supporting the Safety and Dignity of All

Embracing diversity means playing an active role in supporting the safety and dignity of others and ensuring that they are respected, and making sure that we teach our children to do the same. Regardless of age, we can all be champions for diversity by being aware of the biases that we and others hold and that are ingrained in our schools. Indeed, we have an obligation to speak out when we see or hear comments that are disrespectful to others. (That's an example of the integrity discussed in the previous chapter.)

Consider a student who hears a friend call something "gay" as a put-down. The student has an obligation to respond by telling his or her friend that the terminology is not appropriate. Whether phrased as "That wording is unkind and makes me feel uncomfortable" or "It's not right to put down others," the message to the speaker must be clear. Initiating this kind of "courageous conversation" (Singleton, 2015) isn't easy, but it must be done. This can be a hard lesson to teach because we often say that it's not polite to interrupt others. (The Anti-Defamation League refers to calling out disrespectful talk as "interrupting prejudice.") However, the reality—and this is a message that both children and adults need to learn—is that to hear disrespectful comments without responding is really to affirm their use.

Feedback of this sort is particularly powerful coming from a colleague. Years ago, while standing in the main office at my school, one of my teachers used a highly inappropriate derogatory phrase—"He tried to Jew me down"—in reference to a negotiation she'd had with a salesperson. Before I had a chance to respond, the office secretary did.

"That's not a fair or kind comment, and I find it offensive," she said firmly. "That is *not* the way we should think or talk about others!"

The teacher was surprised by the reaction and clearly felt chastised, quickly issuing an apology. I'd like to think that the interaction changed the teacher's mind and heart, but I can't know that. What I do know is neither the secretary nor I ever heard the teacher make a similar comment again. I was very pleased with the secretary's response and told her so. Creating a milieu in which people feel comfortable confronting the biases and bigotry displayed by others is an important step in teaching how to embrace diversity.

Steps in Teaching Embracing Diversity

There are five steps for teaching students the success skill of *embracing diversity*:

1. Appreciating ourselves
2. Recognizing others' diversities
3. Appreciating others
4. Planning
5. Implementing

Too often educators don't pursue embracing diversity because they see it as beyond their scope, something that is static and not likely to change. In fact, understanding others—embracing diversity—is a success skill that can be developed.

Step 1: Appreciating Ourselves

Students of all ages should begin the process of embracing diversity by reflecting inward. They must learn to understand themselves, starting with their identity (race, ethnicity, socioeconomic status, religion) and progressing to the biases and perspectives that they and their families hold. This sort of reflection provides rich opportunities for students to interview their parents and grandparents, as well as to do some research on their family history. (Note: Biases is intentionally used here because we all have biases. Starting with that position and then identifying the biases and speculating on what may have caused them is much healthier and more productive than denying that they exist.)

Step 2: Recognizing Others' Diversities

As noted earlier, our evolutionary instinct has always been to focus on differences, so recognizing others is going beyond that, and also identifying what we have in common. In doing this, it is both fair and helpful for us to consider the contexts of others—their culture, background, and history as a step in appreciation. Of course, considering context doesn't mean validating behavior that is uncaring or cruel, but many of our differences are no better or worse—just that, *different*.

When we recognize others, we must consider the many aspects of diversity that we all possess. Race is a natural aspect of diversity for us to note because it is so visible, yet there are other aspects of diversity that are just as powerful, although not nearly as salient. The theory of multiple intelligences can be a good tool for helping children appreciate one aspect of the diversity of diversities that we all have. People learn and engage in tasks differently depending on their type of intelligence—a fact that resonates with students. We also need to be sure that students go beyond the superficial and realize that each person contains a diversity of diversities; we are all different in different ways.

Step 3: Appreciating Others

Appreciating others can be difficult due to our tendency to judge everyone through a prism; it also requires time and empathy (see Chapter 2). To begin, we need to focus on the strengths of people who are different from us—those who look different than we do, those from different cultures, and those with different attitudes. Setting aside our contexts and biases, we need to seek to understand how these people are appreciated by the others around them. It is during this step that *embracing* becomes a reality. Hopefully students learn not only to understand and respect the differences among us but to appreciate and embrace them, too. After all, group outings, parties, and sports teams are more fun and more productive when the participants represent a diversity of diversities (true for adults too!). Bringing this reality to life in our schools, making it more than just something we read and talk about, is the best way to help children understand and appreciate the differences among us.

Steps 4 and 5: Planning and Implementing

Like the steps for the similarly intrapersonal formative skill of empathy, those for embracing diversity require us to thoughtfully—with intent—interact with others. The final two steps in teaching for the embracing of diversity, planning and implementing, are designed to enable students to act upon the understanding and respect they have for one another—first in the classroom, then schoolwide, and finally in the greater community. We want students to see themselves as active participants in embracing diversity, people who have an opportunity—an obligation—to make the world better by how they understand and relate to others. Class discussions and projects can focus on this, individually and collectively, and then students get to work by implementing. Though this may sound like a tall order—and it is!—it's only natural that as students learn to embrace diversity themselves, they'll want to help others do the same. (For more information, consult the Southern Poverty Law Center's "Teaching Tolerance" website at www.tolerance.org. Particularly helpful is their Anti-Bias Framework, a set of anchor standards and age-appropriate learning outcomes divided into four domains: identity, diversity, justice, and action).

Pursuing diversity isn't easy. As Eboo Patel, founder and president of Interfaith Youth Core, stated: "Diversity is not just about the differences you like." Embracing diversity means getting out of our comfort zones and offering respect and appreciation for diversities that may run counter to our beliefs. For example, I have heard many times recently about people who were once unalterably opposed to GLBT rights doing a complete turnaround once a family member of theirs was coming out. While it is good that they changed their position, embracing diversity doesn't require that someone we care about belongs to a subjugated minority.

Considering Both the Formal and Informal Curriculum

As we think about turning embracing diversity into a norm, we need to consider both the formal and informal curriculum. To some degree, if our students are going to learn and practice embracing diversity, this needs to be a planned part of formal lessons, classroom activities, and school experiences. Whether it's a lesson about the U.S. internment camps for those of Japanese ancestry during World War II or examining Westward Expansion from the perspective of Native Americans, we need to consider how aspects of diversity can be uncovered, included, and embraced in the classroom.

At the same time, we cannot overlook the informal curriculum—the ethos and attitudes found in a school. As I note in *The Art of School Leadership*:

> The informal curriculum consists of the routines, the practices, the policies, and the cultures that guide our behavior; it is what we *do*. We may teach that the U.S. Constitution says that all men are created equal, but what do our actions say about how we value individuals who are gay or lesbian? We may say that the Holocaust was a terrible event, but does our school accept and support a range of religious beliefs, and is this respect evident when looking at events and holidays in the school calendar? We might say that we value human diversity, but what do the papers and work samples on the bulletin boards and walls say about which kinds of students and behaviors are esteemed? We may say that all individuals warrant respect, but are all the members of our staff treated with equal dignity? These kinds of examples represent the informal curriculum. Although it isn't written anywhere, the informal curriculum guides attitudes and behavior. The messages sent by the informal curriculum are very obvious, and regardless of their age, students are savvy at watching what we say and comparing it to what we do. (Hoerr 2005, p. 143)

It is certainly important to consider the informal curriculum for each of the Formative Five skills. We need to be aware of how everything we say and do reinforces our formal efforts to support and develop empathy, self-control, integrity, and grit. But because of the unique position of embracing diversity as an undervalued skill and because of our history and our biases, we need to be particularly vigilant to ensure that we aggressively support diversity with our words and actions.

Finally, while pursuing each of the Formative Five requires communication, inclusion, and informing students' parents and colleagues about what we are doing, it is even more important when working to embrace diversity. The sometimes tepid responses or even opposition that this success skill may elicit make it critical to explain, explain again, and explain once more why this skill is important for our students.

Strategies for Developing the Skill of Embracing Integrity

For all teachers:

- **Refer to the Southern Poverty Law Center's Teaching Tolerance blog at www.teachingtolerance.org.** In addition to articles, this rich resource is full of ideas, activities, and lessons.
- **Ensure that the people and characters discussed in class or portrayed on school walls represent a wide spectrum of demographic variables.** All students need to see that people who look like them have been successful.
- **Create mixed-variable learning groups so that students work with classmates who are both like and unlike them.** This strategy works against our tendency to be most comfortable among people who are similar to us. Finding occasions for students to work in mixed-grade teams can likewise help students embrace age diversity.

For elementary teachers:

- **Create a chart of students' skin colors using crayons, peanut butter, and pudding to show the continuum of various shades.** You can also mix milk and cocoa in different cups, matching each one to the colors. We have done this in kindergarten at my school for years, and students and parents find it both fun and educational. Treating skin color this way demystifies it and helps children understand that color is pigment and nothing more. Posting the chart and an explanation in the hall can lead to rich conversations among other students, students' parents, and visitors.

• **Begin by examining characters from animated movies, since they're entirely fabricated, and asking students to identify any stereotypes they see.** This is an easy and fun way to raise students' awareness about stereotypes, which we can easily take for granted.

• **Ask students to identify stereotypes in other movies and in books.** Ask, "Do the stereotypes allow us to predict how characters will behave? How have stereotypes changed over time? How might others stereotype us?"

• **Bring packages to be unwrapped—one in bright paper with a bow on it, and another in newspaper and masking tape.** Students can talk about how the wrapping has no relationship to the contents. Depending upon the age of the children, the discussion can lead to considering parallel situations in life.

• **Conduct or discuss Jane Elliott's Blue Eyes Brown Eyes exercise (discussed in Chapter 2).** Ask, "How would you feel? How is this relevant today?"

• **Read *Red: A Crayon's Story* by Michael Hall to students.** This book depicts a crayon that is red but feels blue inside, which makes it ideal for discussing transgender children or others who feel different than the way they are seen.

• **Read Barbara Thomson's book, *Words Can Hurt You: Beginning a Program of Anti-Bias Education* (1992).** Barbara, one-time director of diversity for the New City School, offers many lesson plans for embracing diversity.

For middle and high school teachers:

• **Ask students to bring a newspaper or magazine clipping to class that they feel shows an example of discrimination.** Students can then engage in debate, with some taking the side of the discriminated group and others of those doing the discriminating—for five minutes.

Then have students switch positions and argue from the other perspective. The goal is to help students step out of their experiences and understand the thinking of others, even when it is flawed. The importance of listening should be emphasized, especially when students disagree with another's position.

- **Examine the demographics and attendant implications of the local community with your students.** This strategy lends itself best to social students and math classes. A good resource from the U.S. Census Bureau can be found here: http://factfinder.census.gov.

- **Focus on embracing diversity as another way to end bullying.** It's important for students to understand that we all have to work against our tendency to favor those who are most like us. As Singal (2016) notes, "If students think their peers enjoy bullying, or at least aren't opposed to it, they'll be more likely to not just engage in bullying themselves, but also to fail to intervene when they see other people doing it." To work against this tendency, Singal reports that researchers selected popular middle school students—whom they termed "influencers"—and asked them to spread anti-bullying messages. These efforts led to a 30 percent reduction in conflicts among students in the study. (The sample size was more than 24,000 students.)

- **Ask students to read and discuss Natalie Angier's 2013 article for the *New York Times Magazine* "The Changing American Family."** In it, Natalie Angier says that families in the United States "are more ethnically, racially, religiously and stylistically diverse than half a generation ago—than even half a year ago." She goes on to note that today's "birthrate is half of what it used to be . . . [and] maternity is often decoupled from matrimony: 40 percent of women with some college but no degree, and 57 percent of women with a high school education or less, are unmarried when they give birth to their first child."

As Gold (2016) says, "We naturally sort people and experiences into familiar categories that fit past experiences. Acknowledging this human tendency with students can open up a conversation about how stereotypes are used in society. Building on the idea of how power factors into stereotyping, students can see then how certain stereotypes have been used to harm or limit groups while others have had little effect or are even deemed positive."

- **Have students read and discuss Rachel L. Swarns's 2016** *New York Times* **article, "272 Slaves Were Sold to Georgetown University. What Does It Owe Their Descendants?"** Ask them what similar historical responsibilities might apply to your school, city, or state. A subsequent article by Swarns, explaining how Georgetown is responding, can subsequently be discussed. (Both articles are noted in References.)

For principals:

- **Formally appoint someone to a part-time or full-time position as your school's diversity champion.** As I wrote in my April 2016 *Educational Leadership* column, "Every school needs a diversity champion, someone who lives, breathes, and proselytizes diversity. The key qualification for this role—and it should have a title so that there is accountability and no confusion—is passion for [diversity] issues" (Hoerr, 2016b).
- **Routinely highlight diversity at faculty meetings.** Regularly addressing diversity issues sends a powerful message. Although bringing in outside experts and watching videos is always valuable, it's important to begin by helping employees—I use that term because these efforts should not be limited to teachers and administrators—examine their experiences and attitudes about diversity. The principal could do this by asking people to begin with a minute of silent reflection before gathering to discuss the following questions in groups of four or fewer:
  - When you were in elementary school, how aware were you of diversity?
  - Did your family celebrate any religious holidays when you were growing up? What about today?
  - Can you remember ever feeling discriminated against?
  - What stereotypes exist about a group of which you are a member?
  - What stereotypes do you hold about other groups?
  - How do you bring your diversity history to your role at the school?

These discussions can be difficult, perhaps even painful, so the principals need to explain their value—"We are going to reflect on our identities so that we can work from there to help our students"—and ensure respect for all participants. Particularly when interactions can be hard, it's worthwhile to end the meeting with a positive focus by asking people to reflect for a minute on what they learned, and then share in a small group.

• **Create a faculty diversity committee.** This group might be charged with helping to plan professional development offerings on diversity issues and could be the venue for an ongoing book group. At my school, we have used our committee to discuss books that feature a diversity of diversities: *Warriors Don't Cry* (1994), by Melba Pattillo Beals; *Quiet* (2012), by Susan Cain; *The Absolutely True Diary of a Part-Time Indian* (2007), by Sherman Alexie; and *Battle Hymn of the Tiger Mother* (2011), by Amy Chua, among others. (It would be powerful for the administrator to be an active member of this committee; *not* to do so also sends a powerful message.)

• **Show the Ad Council video *Love Has No Labels* (2015) at a faculty meeting.** Afterward, ask faculty to break into small groups and discuss how they reacted when they first saw the identities of the people behind the screen. Then ask about the benefits of showing this video to their students. (The video is available here: www.youtube.com/watch?v=PnDgZuGIhHs.)

• **Show the BBC video *Crossing a St. Louis Street That Divides Communities* (2012) at a faculty meeting.** This video shows how Delmar Boulevard serves as a dividing line between a largely black and poor neighborhood and a largely wealthy and white one in St. Louis. Some questions that might elicit good conversations include, "What might be a comparable street in our city?" "What caused such a divide?" and "How should schools respond to these different circumstances?"

• **Use the Race Card Project to heighten school-wide understanding of and appreciation for diversity issues.** Created by former NPR commentator Michele Norris, the activity asks people to share their thoughts about race with just six words. The faculty, the board of trustees, and upper-grade students at New City School have all taken part in this project. We invited everyone to share his or her six words on three-by-five cards that we posted to a bulletin board in the front hall, near the main office door. The emotions that can be presented in six words are quite powerful, and can lead to candid and rich discussions. Here are examples of some of the race cards that our 5th graders created:

> Please look me in the eye
> Crossing streets define this Missouri city
> You are not like the others
> Chips on shoulders weigh a lot
> Not white enough, not black enough

More information about the project, including samples of many adults' race cards and an opportunity to submit your own, is available at www .theracecardproject.com.

- **Invite a panel of parents to attend a faculty meeting and discuss what diversity means to them.** The demographic makeup of the panels will vary depending on your school's needs. I've convened panels of exclusively black parents and also of parents of adopted children. It was moving and instructive to hear people talking about diversity from their personal perspectives and sharing times when they had felt discrimination. Too often, we talk around race rather than addressing it directly; hearing from members of a panel removes the façade and facilitates candor.

- **Ensure that all genders have equal chances to succeed and be recognized.** It would be worthwhile to compare students' participation rates by gender in student government, athletics, and other school activities and competitions. In doing this, be sure to consider how your school can support transgendered students. Representatives from Gender Spectrum, a San Francisco–based transgender advocacy group, have twice delivered effective presentations to faculty and parents and spoken with students at New City School.

Books That Support the Development of Embracing Diversity Among Students

Picture books:

- *Mixed Me!* (2015), by Taye Diggs (illustrations by Shane W. Evans)
- *Shades of Black* (2006), by Sandra L. Pinkney and Myles C. Pinkney
- *The Other Side* (2001), by Jacqueline Woodson (illustrations by E. B. Lewis)
- *Just Kidding* (2006), by Trudy Ludwig (illustrations by Adam Gustavson)

Chapter books:

- *Wonder* (2012), by R. J. Palacio
- *George* (2015), by Alex Gino
- *Totally Joe* (2007), by James Howe
- *Speak to Me (and I Will Listen Between the Lines)* (2004), by Karen English
- *Kimchi and Calamari* (2010), by Rose Kent
- *Firegirl* (2007), by Tony Abbott
- *Awkward* (2015), by Svetlana Chmakova

Because this success skill may require additional focus, here are suggestions of books for and faculty discussion groups.

- *The Rebellious Life of Mrs. Rosa Parks* (2014), by Jeanne Theoharis
- *Between the World and Me* (2015), by Ta-Nehisi Coates
- *Warriors Don't Cry* (1994), by Melba Pattillo Beals
- *Whistling Vivaldi and Other Clues to How Stereotypes Affect Us* (2010), by Carl Steele
- *The Grace of Silence* (2011), by Michele Norris
- *Sacred Ground* (2013), by Eboo Patel
- *The Invention of Wings* (2014), by Sue Monk Kidd
- *Just Mercy: A Story of Justice and Redemption* (2014), by Bryan Stephenson

6

Grit

Success is the ability to go from failure to failure without losing your enthusiasm.

—Winston Churchill

Lukas was a talented kid to whom most things seemed to come fairly naturally. He excelled at just about everything he attempted: he played saxophone in the school band, was a starting shortstop on the varsity baseball team, made the honor roll, and received a second-place ribbon in the citywide student art fair for an image of rain he'd designed on his computer. The one thing Lukas couldn't handle, however, was adversity. When the going got tough, Lukas was gone. For example, despite his considerable athletic skills, he refused to play any position other than shortstop, and he wouldn't try out for any sports other than baseball. When he wasn't named first sax in the band, he quit. Academically, Lukas did well, in part because he spent a lot of time finding out exactly what the teacher sought. His focus was avoiding failure, as even the smallest failure overwhelmed him. Lukas quit participating when he stopped succeeding.

Juanita wasn't the best athlete or the strongest student, but she was the one every coach wanted on the team and every teacher wanted in the classroom. What Juanita may have lacked in scholastic talent or coordination she more than compensated for with her tenacity, perseverance, and resilience. To her, success meant that she was ready for the next challenge. She was all about reducing her time in the mile and raising her score on the test, even though she knew it meant frustration along the way. She was fearless, and she could always generate an extra bit of energy and dose of determination. In a word, Juanita had *grit*. She never gave up and pushed herself not just to realize her potential but to perform better than anyone could reasonably expect.

Figure 6.1 shows the self-assessment survey for *grit*. Take a moment to answer the questions before continuing with this chapter.

What Is Grit?

As I note in *Fostering Grit* (2013a), grit is tenacity, perseverance, hanging in, and not ever giving up. In an NPR interview, Angela Duckworth calls grit a "combination of passion and perseverance for very long-term goals" (NPR staff, 2015).

Grit is found all around us; it is a factor in just about everyone's against-the-odds success. When you talk to people who've "made it" (however that is defined), they invariably talk about how their accomplishments stem from their failure to give up and their ability to hang in—their tenacity, or grit. Occasionally, grit is even featured in the entertainment industry. Have you read Laura Hillenbrand's *Unbroken* (2010) or seen the film adaptation? The story is both inspiring and daunting. If it were a fictional account, we'd say that it was too far-fetched to be believable. However, *Unbroken* is the true story of Louis Zamperini, a 1936 Olympic athlete who was also an Army Air Corps bombardier in World War II. His life is a testament to grit: he survived on a life raft for 47 days in the Pacific Ocean after his plane was shot down and was held captive in a Japanese prisoner-of-war camp for years. Whether challenged by fellow athletes, ocean tides, sharks, or prison guards, Zamperini refused to be defeated. He may have never used the word *grit*, but he embodied it.

FIGURE 6.1

Self-Assessment Survey: Grit

Note: The following survey is designed to provide a sense of your feelings about grit. It is a tool to elicit reflection and discussion, not a scientifically valid instrument.

Directions: Place a 1 (strongly disagree), 2 (disagree), 3 (not sure), 4 (agree), or 5 (strongly agree) after each item.

1. Intellect determines success. ____

2. Students should always have chances to redo assignments. ____

3. Students' trajectories should help determine their grades. ____

4. My goal is to have happy students. ____

5. In my professional life, I often succeed because I don't give up. ____

6. Students lose confidence when they fail. ____

7. When things get hard for me, I find myself distracted. ____

8. In my personal life, I often succeed because I don't give up. ____

9. Non-cognitive skills are mostly developed outside of school. ____

10. I am comfortable sharing my mistakes and what I've learned from them. ____

Scoring:

____ (A) Total points for 2, 3, 5, 8, 10

____ (B) Total points for 1, 4, 6, 7, 9

____ (C) Subtract (B) from (A) for your "grit" score

If you scored

- *18 or higher:* You fully understand the issue of grit!

- *15–17:* You understand grit but may need to work more directly on it with your students.

- *12–14:* You should probably focus more on grit in your classroom instruction.

- *11 or lower:* You would probably benefit from reading up on or joining a discussion group about grit.

Note: You can find a grit self-assessment survey for students in Appendix A.

Fortunately, we're not likely to face the challenges Zamperini surmounted, but we will need grit nonetheless in our lives—and we need to develop it in our students. In all endeavors, the achievements of highly successful people do not come easily, regardless of how effortless they may appear. They possess their skills, talents, and acumen because they work diligently, persevering constantly to improve; they refuse to give up and are unwilling to settle for anything less than success. They encounter frustrations and failures along the way, but they see them as obstacles, not walls. In the words of Jon Sinclair, people who achieve do so because they know that "Failure is a bruise. Not a tattoo."

Thinking about failure as being associated with success may appear counterintuitive. After all, we recognize the grace and natural ease that is obvious in the performance of highly successful people. Whether it's admiring a pianist as his hands dance across the keyboard, applauding a basketball player as she dribbles behind her back, or appreciating a poet as she brings words to life, we are in awe of both the skills on display and on how naturally they seem to be delivered. It seems as if the people we're admiring were born being able to perform at a high level. In the workplace, we see executives who balance myriad demands, make hard choices, get the job done, and connect with people throughout the organization. "What a gift they have," we think. "Their success comes so effortlessly!" Of course, that's completely wrong. The dexterity that is apparent in their success is the result of hours and hours of effort and responding to setbacks—grit.

Accounts of Grit

Bonnie Barczykowski, the chief executive officer of the Girl Scouts of Eastern Missouri, says, "The greatest accomplishments in my career weren't the 'quick wins' but rather the ones that took resolve, determination and a few failures along the way" (personal communication, January 19, 2016).

Likewise, Elizabeth Towner, a psychologist at Wayne State University who does research on eating disorders, says, "My current position as a researcher is a constant test of my grit. My job depends on getting grants, and I am competing with hundreds of other scientists for a super-tiny pot of money. In my career path, even the most talented scientists are likely to only have one or two grants funded for every dozen that they submit. If I let every rejection knock me down, I'd have quit a long time ago" (personal communication, January 18, 2016).

Sharonica Hardin, the superintendent of the University City School District in St. Louis, says,

> My educational and personal journey is one that truly represents grit. As a teenager, I overcame significant obstacles and persevered despite criticism from others, including some adults. Educationally, I always consider myself a work in progress. I relish the opportunity to learn from and with amazingly smart and talented people of all walks of life. I am an individual who has learned immensely from my failures. Grit is what helps to shape who I am and how I show up every day for the children and adults that I serve. (personal communication, January 19, 2016)

Another powerful example of grit comes from Jeff Lowell, an organ transplant surgeon at St. Louis Children's Hospital (personal communication, January 24, 2016):

> Staring into the deep, dark hole on the left of the upper abdomen, after the life-requiring liver has been removed during the transplant procedure, the clock starts. One hour to get the replacement liver sewn in. Go. Not infrequently lots of complicating, perhaps impossible confabulators arise—the patient's low blood pressure, low or high heart rate, lack of blood clotting; environmental stresses such as noise, very high operating-room temperatures (to help promote blood clotting) and very cold hands (as ice is placed on the liver and in the abdomen to help keep the transplanted liver metabolically inactive until blood has been returned to it); and fatigue (most commonly in the middle of the night). All of these variables conspire against you and your patient. At times they can seem impossible to surmount.

But I will.

Fight. Move. Act. Among the many factors that successfully bring the entire transplant team together is being time-sensitive: getting things done one by one, sucking it up, focusing, drawing on your training and experience, and moving forward with purpose.

Blood restored. Cold, shrunken gray replacement liver has in just a few heart-beats become pink, fully healthy, and functioning. Breathe.

"What's next?"

Former professional basketball player Bob Pettit is another example. Many years ago, when the Hawks still played in St. Louis, Pettit was their star player; indeed, he was one of the top two or three players in the NBA. I attended a number of Hawks games, and it was always a treat to see Pettit perform his magic on the court. Whenever I saw the team play, regardless of whether they won or lost, it was obvious to everyone that Pettit was a gifted athlete, someone to whom playing basketball came naturally. He was so skilled that it almost seemed that he wasn't working that hard.

But there's more to his story.

At the time, I was friends with a woman whose father worked for the St. Louis Police Department. He was responsible for securing the auditorium where the Hawks' home games were held after everyone left. My friend complained about how late her dad would come home on game nights—usually after midnight.

It turns out that after each home game, after the fans had left and after the rest of the players had showered and gone home, Pettit would inevitably return to the court and spend an hour alone, methodically shooting hoops. One of the best players in the league spent an hour refining his skills after everyone else had gone home. Pettit clearly possessed physical talent, but his focus and effort are what made him exceptional.

Similarly, Michael Jordan, arguably the best basketball player of all time, talks about grit when he says, "Obstacles don't have to stop you.

If you run into a wall, don't turn around and give up. Figure out how to climb it, go through it, or work around it."

In a 2016 *New York Times* column by Adam Bryant, an interview with Anthony Foxx, the U.S. transportation secretary, affirms this focus. Foxx discusses what he seeks when he hires: "I'd rather hire someone who's maybe not a genius, but they will dig in on any assignment. I'd rather have resilience than almost any other quality. Competence is obviously critical, but a lot of people who are really smart actually end up walking away from some pretty tough assignments because they're worried about whether they can do them or not."

In reflecting on the role that grit has played in his career, jazz pianist Peter Martin notes:

> When done well, the art of jazz improvisation comes off to the listener as a thrilling and honest artistic expression of the human condition, effortlessly channeled through the artist's instrument live and in the moment. And that's as it should be, as we are first and foremost entertainers. However, the skill set required to effectively improvise in the moment and not have it sound like random notes is quite detailed and involved. A complete technical command of one's instrument, advanced ear training, and a knowledge base of thousands of tunes, riffs, and chords are just some of the prerequisites to becoming a capable jazz performer. And the only way to acquire these skills is countless hours in the practice room. The painful part is listening to yourself for the hundreds of hours it takes until it starts to sound OK, and that's where having grit comes in to play. Because if you don't have the perseverance to push through the difficult skill acquisition period of tortured sounding improvisation, you'll never get to the promised land of being on the bandstand and having a shot at delivering a thrilling live jazz improvisation. And if you make it there, then you've got a chance to showcase your "talent" and make some magic happen for you and the audience. (personal communication, February 3, 2016)

What successful surgeons, athletes, poets, musicians, broadcasters, moms, dads, researchers, and educators all have in common is *grit*. Having grit means possessing an attitude that embraces challenges, willingly stepping out of the comfort zone, and never giving up. Angela Duckworth, the professor whose work pushed grit to public consciousness, defines it as "the tendency to sustain interest in and effort toward very long-term goals" (Duckworth, Peterson, Matthews, & Kelly, 2007). The long-term aspect is integral to Duckworth's definition, and while agreeing with her, I focus more on developing students' shorter-term grit to teach this attitude.

My Journey Toward Grit

My journey toward grit began on the football field at Roosevelt High School in St. Louis when I was a high school freshman. Playing on an organized team and performing publicly for the first time in my life, I was pushed to go way beyond my comfort zone, failed, was embarrassed, failed again, became frustrated—and continued trying. To this day, I can see and feel the opposing tackle humiliating me as I tried to block him, but I also remember knowing that I could not give up. (Thank you, Coach Rogers!)

I was never as good of a football player as I wished (or as I remember!), but I definitely became better through my perseverance, and the lessons I learned back then carried over to other challenges in my life. Later, I became a better student, teacher, and principal because of the grit that I began to learn on that football field, even though at the time I wasn't fully aware of what was happening. (In retrospect, I know that my learning trajectory and pace would have been much better if I had been conscious of grit and its benefits.)

Decades after my football experiences, I gained a renewed appreciation for grit when I read Paul Tough's 2011 article in *New York Times Magazine*, "What If the Secret to Success Is Failure?" Tough wrote about noncognitive skills and cited Duckworth's research on the importance of grit. For example, he noted that she examined students who, though academically prepared for college, had their progress there halted due to difficulty coping with life challenges (e.g., family crises, difficulties with a teacher, the social pressures of college life). Duckworth identified grit as a key factor in whether or not students could overcome these challenges. She found that the students with grit were far more likely to succeed in school and those without it were at a much greater risk of dropping out. (See Duckworth explain her thinking and research here: www.ted.com /talks/angela_lee_duckworth_the_key_to_success_grit.html.) Tough also wrote about how a student's low score on the "grit test" (a self-scoring inventory created by Duckworth) was a better predictor of who would drop out of the United States Military Academy at West Point than grade point averages or test results. (Tough further explores the importance of grit, as well as the value of other success skills, in his books, *How Children Succeed* [2012] and *Helping Children Succeed* [2016].)

Tough's description of Duckworth's work resonated with me. For some time, I had been talking and writing about success in life versus success in school, and the concept of grit fed my concern that in focusing on standardized tests and limiting ourselves to traditional academics, we fall short in preparing students with the skills and attitudes they will need after they graduate. In short order, I wrote two columns for *Educational Leadership* on the topic of grit: "Got Grit?" (2012) and "Good Failures" (2013b).

Teaching for Grit

Simply put, teaching for grit begins with educators embracing a new attitude toward both student and teacher success. No longer can we judge ourselves simply on how many of our students do well academically, on the smiles that they give us, or on the accolades we receive from parents and peers. These things make us feel good, but they are not sufficient.

Don't misunderstand me: Students should do well in school, they should give us hugs and high-fives to show their satisfaction, and parents and peers should be pleased. But there's more because when you teach for grit, you have different goals; you change what is on the scorecard.

Beyond focusing on academics and curriculum content, teaching for grit means that you're also addressing *attitudes* about what it takes to succeed. Focusing on the importance of grit is not to minimize potential or talent. Rather, it's to indicate that any potential that we possess remains just potential unless we work relentlessly to improve, persevering through failures and frustrations.

To quote Brené Brown (2015), "there can be no innovation, learning, or creativity without failure" (p. xxv). Grit gives us the courage to take risks and to fail because we know that failure is a necessary ingredient in ultimate success. Brown again,

> If we're going to put ourselves out there and love with our whole hearts, we're going to experience heartbreak. If we're going to try new, innovative things, we're going to fail. If we're going to risk caring and engaging, we're going to experience disappointment. It doesn't matter if our hurt is caused by a painful breakup or we're struggling with something smaller, like an offhand comment by a colleague or an argument with an in-law. If we can learn how to feel our way through these experiences and own our own stories of struggle, we can write our own brave endings. (p. xx)

Parents intuitively understand that it is important for their children to develop grit. This was made very clear to me when I shared my enthusiasm about grit in one of my weekly family newsletters. Despite my efforts to make my newsletters interesting and humorous (at least in my opinion), I rarely received feedback on what I wrote. But parent after parent after parent responded by expressing support for our school's efforts to develop grit in their children. Subsequently I offered a Parent Education Evening on grit (and it was attended by so many families that we needed to bring in extra chairs!).

Grit in Education

Grit has been a very hot topic in education for several years now. I've made numerous presentations on the subject in schools, at educational conferences, and to work groups. My 2013 book *Fostering Grit* has been well received and has generated lots of discussion about what educators can do to help their students develop grit. Many educators recognize that it's not enough to teach students to master content; we must also teach them to hang in when things are tough. That's particularly important in today's "trophy society," a climate that embraces positive reinforcement almost irrespective of performance.

Grit is more complex than it might appear to be, and educators need to emphasize "good grit" and "smart grit." Teaching good grit means that we should ensure that students use grit for the right purposes. Smart grit means that we need to teach students to recognize those times when stopping the pursuit of a goal is wise because the gain is not worth the cost.

Criticism of Focusing on Grit as a Formative Skill

There has also been a pushback against grit. Surprisingly, some take emphasizing grit to mean we should ignore external factors that can contribute strongly to student outcomes. Tyrone C. Howard, the associate dean for equity and inclusion at UCLA, says: "We are asking students to change a belief system without changing the situation around them" (Sullivan, 2015). The article also notes that Howard said, "It can be irresponsible and unfair to talk about grit without talking about structural challenges . . . referring to the recent interest in interventions tied to the concepts of grit and perseverance" (Sullivan, 2015).

Similarly, in an *Education Week* article titled "Is Grit Racist?" Benjamin Herold alleges that developing grit "has harmed low-income students by crowding out a focus on providing children with the supports they deserve and the more-flexible educational approach enjoyed by many of their more affluent counterparts" (2015). I responded to the article in an open letter to the editor, noting that grit is important for *everyone*. (You can read my response here: www.newcityschool.org /uploads/miscellaneous/Grit.EW.both.pdf.)

I appreciate that some students come to us from challenging situations, and I understand that too often schools and school systems fail to understand or meet students' needs. We cannot ignore the difficult circumstances in which some children live and the impact that this has on them. But *all* students benefit from having grit; regardless of whether a student is on the honor roll or struggling, she gains when she is able to continue her efforts and resist the temptation to give up. Fostering grit is not a zero-sum game that requires us to ignore the development of other skills in students. As Mike Fleetham of the Thinking Classroom notes, "Many students from low-[socioeconomic] backgrounds are naturally gritty (they've had to be). Our challenge now is to respect and apply this characteristic to academic learning" (personal communication, December 12, 2015).

One valid concern about developing grit is that doing so can run counter to a belief that students should enjoy school as much as possible. Not surprisingly, it is difficult for teachers and principals who have spent their careers finding ways for students to succeed to now embrace that some degree of frustration and failure is necessary so that students can learn how to persevere. And formal teacher and principal evaluations notwithstanding, the reality is that we judge our success as educators on whether our students succeed. But because we understand the importance of fostering grit, we must get beyond a naïve mindset that says our focus should only be on ensuring that students do well on tests. It is in our students' interests for us to occasionally create learning roadblocks so that they can learn, under our guidance and with our care, how to respond when they fall short of expectations. After all, what better place is there for students to meet frustration than in a school setting where they are cared for?

Of course, for many students, learning roadblocks occur naturally. Our task then is to teach them how to develop the grit they need to overcome the challenges they face. This is easier said than done. Some students have learned to ignore frustrations and accept failures. They don't use grit because they don't see success as a realistic possibility. For these students, we need to teach grit in small steps, helping them see how it can benefit them in areas besides school. We can also help them see how the grit they use in other areas—perhaps caring for a younger sibling or pursuing art, music, or sports—can be transferred to scholastic tasks.

In contrast, students for whom school is a series of unbridled successes require more dramatic measures. Duckworth notes that in a study on Ivy League undergraduates, "SAT scores and grit were, in fact, inversely correlated" (2016, p. 14). For these students, it is essential that we engineer frustrations and failures so that they can learn to respond to them. Learning grit is like learning anything else: You learn it by doing it. I've told my faculty that if a student graduates from our school without failing at something, then we have failed that student. (You may not be surprised to learn that this comment created a bit of controversy at first, but it also led to many rich discussions about success, learning, and our roles as educators.) Whether students are struggling in or coasting through school, one thing is certain: They all need our unwavering care, support, and encouragement.

Angela Duckworth described four psychological assets shared by people with lots of grit:

1. Interest—"you can't be gritty about something that you're not interested in"

2. Capacity to engage in deliberate practice—"knowing what deliberate practice is and what it's not and being willing to do it"

3. A sense of purpose—"of how what they do, day in, day out, is meaningful and beneficial to people who are not them"

4. Hope—"the hope to keep going when hope seems lost" (NPR staff, 2015)

I see no contradiction between fostering grit and eliciting smiles. I endorse educators pursuing grit with their students despite the fact that the school I led for decades had "joyful learning" as one of its four pillars. I believe that school should be fun, and that balancing grit with joyful learning is possible when we approach grit as a dialogue—something that is done *with* students and *with* their parents, not done *to* them.

The Steps to Developing Grit

In *Fostering Grit* (Hoerr, 2013a), I identify six steps for developing this crucial formative skill in students:

1. Establishing the environment
2. Setting expectations
3. Teaching the vocabulary
4. Creating frustration
5. Monitoring the experience
6. Reflecting and learning

These steps can be applied regardless of students' age, subject matter, or school context. The sequence creates a setting in which students can take risks, be frustrated, and even fail, all within a context of trust and care. In each of these steps, we must remember that fostering grit is a dialogue: we must be sure to communicate what we are doing and why to students and their parents. Gaining grit stems from collaborative efforts by teachers and students (even if it doesn't feel like this to the student when he is in the middle of a frustrating experience).

Step 1: Establishing the Environment

The school environment has two components: physical and psychological. Physically, schools should celebrate students' progress, positive trajectories, and tenacity. There's definitely a place for highlighting success by displaying championship trophies, the names of national merit semifinalists, and the honor roll, but there should also be room for applauding effort and progress. On sports teams, for example, why not accompany the Most Valuable Player award with one for Most Improved Player or Most Gritty Player? Why not recognize students who have made the biggest gains throughout the semester regardless of where they rank? Physical recognition of progress—what's in the halls and on the walls?—and achievement specific to each of the eight intelligences is critical as well.

Psychologically, the school community should embrace grit and celebrate stick-to-it-iveness. Teachers and principals should note its importance at graduation ceremonies, back-to-school nights, and faculty meetings. Consider the following comment from Desiree, the parent of a student at New City School in St. Louis, Missouri: "Grit has given me, as a parent, a different perspective on my daughter's learning difficulties. In the long run, my hope is that she'll be a stronger person who appreciates the rewards her hard work has brought and apply her grittiness to all aspects of her life." We also must commend educators who have shown grit. And because we measure what we value, we must carefully think about how we might reflect students' grit on report cards.

Step 2: Setting Expectations

Educators need to take the lead in reminding everyone—students, parents, sometimes even colleagues and administrators—that learning to respond well to frustration and failure is a pivotal life skill. Of course, this means that *we* must experience frustration and failure ourselves. We need to step outside of our comfort zones and consciously work to develop our grit. Establishing the expectation that grit is important means that I focused on it in faculty meetings and parent communications. In my weekly family newsletters, I often included quotes by famous people that spoke to the importance of grit and links to articles on the subject. At faculty meetings, I sometimes asked teachers to meet in small groups and discuss what they had done to develop grit in their students. Teachers also talked about the importance of grit with their students and students' parents.

Step 3: Teaching the Vocabulary

We must be able to describe grit in various ways so that we can recognize the skill in different contexts. *Tenacity, resilience, pluck, stick-to-it-iveness, backbone, guts, courage, bravery, resoluteness, intrepidness,* and *spunk* are all terms with meanings very similar to *grit*. It's helpful for students to routinely use these terms when they plan and reflect on their efforts. Educators must note the differences among the terms as well, specifying that grit refers specifically to overcoming frustration or failure.

One oxymoronic term that I use quite often because it is both explanatory and helpfully bumptious is *good failures*. None of us want to fail, but a good failure is one from which we learn. The term conveys the positive attributes of grit and can encourage students to step out of their comfort zones and take risks. (One year I had t-shirts made for faculty with *Good Failures* printed on them; some teachers told me that the shirts led to some good conversations when they wore them out and about in the community.)

Step 4: Creating Frustration

Before teachers intentionally create frustrating experiences for students, it is important that they prepare their students for what they are doing. For example, on a Friday, a teacher might remind the class that Monday is going to be Grit Day, so the classroom tone and expectations will purposely be more challenging than usual. "You're not going to like me much on Monday," the teacher might say, "and that's OK." By the end of Grit Day, most students will be fed up and ready to quit, which is when the teacher can help them reflect on and learn from their challenges.

Our approaches to creating frustrations for students should vary according to their multiple intelligences. At my school, for example, while we use MI to capitalize on kids' strengths, we occasionally work to develop grit by forcing students to use their weakest intelligence when learning or showing what they know.

Sometimes, educators express concern about jeopardizing students' academic standing by teaching them grit; that's a fair concern. But there are creative ways around this worry—from not factoring in the lowest score when averaging grades, to forcing students to use a type of intelligence that isn't graded traditionally, to simply not including grit lessons in the final grade. A student who has never received a grade other than an *A* might be devastated by a *B+*, but the whole point is to teach him or her how to channel disappointment productively.

Step 5: Monitoring the Experience

Strong educators are always monitoring their students' reactions—not only to understand what and how they're learning but to gain an awareness of their attitudes toward learning. Thus, teachers must be cognizant of the moments when their students become frustrated. The time to teach grit is when the student wants to quit! We need to help students realize that the learning journey is very important and that the right attitude can turn a regular failure into a good failure.

Step 6: Reflecting and Learning

After an exercise in grit—when the clouds have parted and the sun is shining again—teachers should ask students to reflect on how they felt throughout the experience. What did they do when they first experienced frustration? How did they respond when they were bored? What did they say to themselves to keep persevering? Most important, what did they learn that they will be able to use the next time they become frustrated or fail at something? As Deb Holmes, retired assistant superintendent from the Kirkwood School District in Missouri, says (personal communication, October 11, 2015), "We all benefit from considering what strengthens our persistence when we are challenged, and we are all challenged."

To help students reflect and compare reactions over time and across experiences, teachers might want to create a classroom rubric chart that allows students to determine their personal level of frustration. Figure 6.2 comes from *Fostering Grit*, but it would be best to use student input in creating one to be visibly hung on a classroom wall. Its presence would facilitate discussions about how students are feeling and responding to frustrations.

FIGURE 6.2		
Frustration Chart		
Frustration Level	**The Work Is . . .**	**How I'm Feeling**
1	Easy	No problem!
2	OK	I'm in good shape.
3	Hard	I'll figure it out.
4	Very difficult	Not sure I can succeed.
5	Too hard!	I want to quit.

Source: Fostering Grit: How do I prepare my students for the real world? (p. 27), by T. R. Hoerr, 2013. Alexandria, VA: ASCD. Copyright 2013 by ASCD.

If we are to successfully foster grit in our students, we must help them become agents in their learning. Regardless of their age, learning isn't something we do *for* or *to* them; rather, learning is something that we do *with* our students—after all, every one of us learns—and our students should be engaged partners in the process.

Strategies for Developing Grit

For all teachers:

• **Have students create a Grit Chart and post it in the classroom.** It could feature famous and not-so-famous people who are known for their grit (e.g., Rosa Parks, Winston Churchill, Charles Darwin, Michael Jordan, Abraham Lincoln). The chart reminds everyone that the most important tasks require grit, and that success is built upon many failures.

• **Introduce and routinely use the term *good failure* so that students can understand that what matters is how they learn from failing.** Students should know that learning from failure makes it less likely to re-occur and helps develop grit.

- **On Friday, tell students that Monday morning's class will begin with them sharing stories of how they used grit over the weekend.** Mentioning this in advance increases the likelihood that students will reflect and internalize the need to develop grit. (Alternatively, teachers might give students advance notice before recess or lunchtime that they'll be asked about grit when they return to class.)
- **Create a "Gritster of the Week" award, complete with a certificate (Figure 6.3).** (Thanks to Mike Fleetham [personal correspondence, December 12, 2015] for this idea.)
- **Working from pretests (or initial tests), ask students to set goals that cause them to stretch and move out of their comfort zone.**
- **Use goal setting as a tool to work toward grit.** Encourage students to see grit as a byproduct of their efforts to stretch themselves and meet goals.
- **Show students Nike's *Failure* commercial featuring Michael Jordan.** You can access the video here: www.youtube.com/watch?v=8HkGmRShkjI.

For elementary teachers

- **Provide specific opportunities for students to learn something new and hard (but fun!) so that they can consciously work on grit as they learn.** Plate-spinning (using plastic plates, of course) is one example; others might include playing an instrument or walking on a low-level balance beam. Though none of these activities may be part of the formal curriculum, they support academic success by developing skills related to grit that students can transfer to their schoolwork.
- **Establish a climate in which grit is often thought about, discussed, and actively pursued.** This example is from Naoimh Campbell, who teaches 5th graders in Leicester, United Kingdom (personal communication, January 2, 2016):

    The children in my class are gritty; their life experience has forced them to be. However, their grit doesn't always translate

---

FIGURE 6.3
Certificate

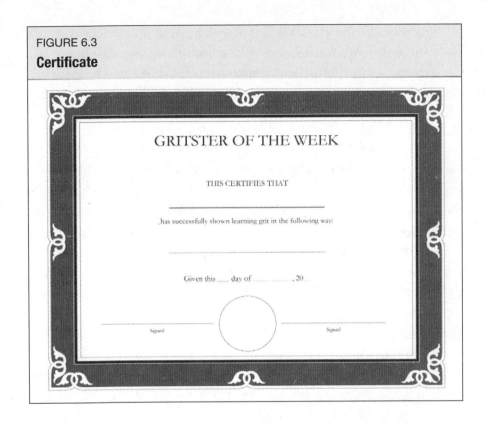

GRITSTER OF THE WEEK

THIS CERTIFIES THAT

_____

.has successfully shown learning grit in the following way:

_____

Given this ____ day of _____ , 20__

Signed   Signed

---

in the academic sense. For some, the classroom is one of the only places they feel safe, it is the only place where structures are not only in place but adhered to. In this sense, their status within the classroom is deeply important to them and failure is not an option. I recognized that the reluctance of some of my most vulnerable children to take risks was having an impact on their learning. I implemented a grit jar, I invited a mascot (Paula the Persevering Panda) and wrote a Grit Assembly which the children performed (complete with gymnastics routine, this required grit from staff and students alike!). I slowly noticed a change in the children's attitude: they had the confidence to sweat over problems that would have previously triggered tears, they supported each other, and they surprised themselves with their ability. We had relapses and tantrums when a new hand-writing scheme pushed everyone to the edge, but a nod towards the grit jar and a few encouraging words often were enough to make even the most risk averse student have a go.

• **Have students interview their parents, family members, or other adults about their experiences with grit.** Students can then share the responses in class. By eliciting multiple responses and categorizing them by diversity (age, gender, etc.), this strategy can double as a logical-mathematical activity.

• **Discuss whether the characters in books or articles are exhibiting grit.** Alternatively, how might plots have evolved differently if one or more of the characters had possessed grit?

For middle or high school teachers:

• **Emphasize the term** *comfort zone.* This strategy is particularly useful with adolescents, who are often especially uncomfortable with failure or standing apart in any way. Teachers should routinely exhort students to get out of their comfort zones.

• **Have students interview people who are good at their jobs to see how much grit contributed to their success.** When interviewing, students shouldn't mention grit at all—the idea is for them to identify instances that are shared by others. This strategy could easily be used in a social studies class examining individuals' roles in the community, or it could be another logical-mathematical exercise in comparing and contrasting different professions.

• **Discuss how the words** *tenacity, resilience, pluck, stick-to-it-iveness, backbone, guts, courage, bravery, resoluteness, intrepidness,* **and** *spunk* **are all related to the idea of grit and what the differences among them are.**

• **Ask high school students to write a letter offering strategies for developing grit in young children.** By purposely focusing on younger children, this strategy requires students to step back and examine how grit is developed.

• **Have students bring in a newspaper article showing an example of grit (even if the word itself isn't used).** Students can post their articles on a Grit Bulletin Board.

• **Ask students whether they think it's fair to note students' efforts and degrees of improvement on report cards.** Should they be considered part of a grade? This should lead to a rich discussion about grit and school (but be prepared to deal with Pandora's Box once it is opened).

For principals:

• **Allocate professional development time for focusing on grit.** Principals might begin by asking faculty to reflect on times when they personally used grit to overcome obstacles. A useful way to open the dialogue might be to determine the faculty's receptivity to grit using the teacher self-assessment survey in Figure 6.1.

• **Ensure that grit is promoted in displays throughout the school.** How are progress, stronger trajectories, and tenacity reflected on walls and in the halls?

• **Routinely use the term** *comfort zone* **in faculty meetings and bulletins.** For example, I once sent the following note to faculty in a weekly school bulletin:

Comfort Zone: Have you used the term with your kids lately? Recall, please, that at my grit presentation, I talked about how we all need to move out of our comfort zones, and that part of this process was explaining the term to your students and to their parents. The goal is for kids to understand and be able to say something like, "This is out of my comfort zone, but I'm going to try it anyway." Likewise, comfort zone is a key factor in our parent education, I am convinced. Please use it in your teaching, in your classroom, and in your Parent Letter.

- **Convene a faculty committee to examine how students' efforts and degrees of improvement are reflected in the report cards and recommend improvements.** Are teachers given opportunities to note grit either in symbols or words? If not, how might they supplement a traditional report? For example, might they insert an additional page within the main report that focuses specifically on growth and effort? With older students, why not spend a class period with them helping them write letter to parents describing how hard they have worked and how they have responded to setbacks?

- **Periodically begin faculty meetings by asking teachers to identify students who have displayed grit.** Principals should try soliciting the names of students who aren't usually the center of positive attention as a reminder that all students need grit. (One way to widen the net of students is to ask teachers of less academic subjects—art, music, physical education—to take the lead. Many of the students who excel in these classes aren't noticed enough in those devoted to languages, science, or mathematics.)

- **Share the following articles about grit with faculty and parents:**
  - "Why Parents Need to Let Their Children Fail" (2013), by Jessica Lahey. *The Atlantic.* Available: www.theatlantic.com/national /archive/2013/01/why-parents-need-to-let-their-children-fail/272603
  - "Good Failures: Great Successes" (2016a), by Thomas R. Hoerr. *Independent School.*
  - "The Trouble with Bright Kids" (2011) by Heidi Grant Halvorson. *Harvard Business Review.* Available: https://hbr.org/2011/11 /the-trouble-with-bright-kids

Books That Support the Development of Grit

Picture books:

- *Flight School* (2014), by Lita Judge
- *Giraffes Can't Dance* (2012), by Giles Andreae (illustrations by Guy Parker-Rees)
- *Mirette on the High Wire* (1997), by Emily Arnold McCully

- *The Most Magnificent Thing* (2014), by Ashley Spires
- *Sally Jean, Bicycle Queen* (2006), by Cari Best (illustrations by Christine Davenier)
- *Thank You, Mr. Falker* (2012), by Patricia Polacco

Chapter books:

- *Letters from Rifka* (2009), by Karen Hesse
- *Hatchet* (2006), by Gary Paulsen

7

Culture Is the Key

The school's culture dictates, in no uncertain terms, the way we do things around here.

—Roland Barth

This book is about preparing students for the real world by teaching them the Formative Five success skills: *empathy, self-control, integrity, embracing diversity,* and *grit.* It is about schools where, in addition to academic skills, students learn how to work with others and to understand themselves. This means that we need to design curriculum, teach, assess, and work with colleagues in ways that encourage the development of the Formative Five. It also means that we must focus directly on school culture. Paul Tough (2016) says, "If we want to improve a child's grit or resilience or self-control, it turns out that the place to begin is not with the child himself. What we need to change first, it seems, is his environment" (p. 12). The environment to which Tough refers is the physical setting, but it is far more than that. It is the expectations, attitudes, and norms surrounding the child—the culture.

The power of an organization's culture—the felt, lived environment of the place—to influence people's perceptions and attitudes and to frame their behaviors cannot be overstated.

"Culture is the common core that creates belonging, influences our behaviors, and shapes who we become," say Curt Coffman and Kathie Sorensen in *Culture Eats Strategy for Lunch* (2013, p. 15). When we visit a school, we can feel its culture within a few minutes. We can feel it even just viewing a school's website (e.g., is it mundane or cluttered, or does it convey an appreciation for students and a sense of excitement?). What impressions do we get? What do we or don't we notice? When we enter the front doors of a school, walk through the halls, and observe the interactions among adults and children, we are feeling the school's culture.

Even if a culture evolved without intent, it will be influential and entrenched. Everyone knows "that's how we do things" even though students and educators come and go. School cultures are remarkably resistant to change. (That said, since the passage of No Child Left Behind, high standardized test results have been much more heavily prioritized over the development of nurturing and creative environments than they used to be. Much of the whole child movement is a reaction to this fact.)

Given an almost maniacal focus on test scores, it's no surprise that most school cultures will need to change—to *evolve*—if they are to support the Formative Five. For years, most schools have focused almost exclusively on teaching academic subjects; further, many schools operated within a largely top-down leadership framework. A focus on the Formative Five success skills requires modifications to the curriculum, new teaching practices, and more evenly distributed leadership throughout the school.

In *The Culture Engine*, Chris Edmonds says, "The most effective culture champions are very specific about their beliefs" (2014, p. 42). It's true that principals have the primary responsibility for creating a school culture, but the reality is far more complex. In every good school, and particularly in those that focus on the Formative Five skills, leadership is distributed among all staff members. Everyone shares responsibilities and feels ownership for the school's progress and success. Ensuring this kind of collaboration isn't easy. As Howard Schultz, the chairman and CEO of Starbucks, says, "Turning a culture around is very difficult to do because it's based on a series of many, many decisions, and the organization is framed by those decisions" (2010). If they are going to be successful in pursuing the Formative Five skills, principals and teachers will need to work together in making those decisions. This doesn't mean that principals should abdicate their roles but, rather, that they should engage faculty and build relationships based on respect and trust. "Trust is the foundation of leadership; if you trust people, they will trust you back" say Bob Chapman and Raj Sosodia in *Everybody Matters* (2015, p. 116).

The Six Components of Culture

In a 2013 *Harvard Business Review* article titled "Six Components of a Great Corporate Culture," John Coleman dissects the six core components:

1. *Mission*—what the organization will do
2. *Values*—guidelines for behaviors
3. *Practices*—how the mission will be achieved
4. *People*—getting, keeping, and developing the right individuals
5. *Narrative*—stories that convey culture
6. *Place*—functionality and appearance

Figure 7.1 shows the questions that each of Coleman's components of culture raises for schools.

Working from the questions in Figure 7.1, here are suggestions and strategies for building a school culture that supports developing the Formative Five success skills.

1: Mission

Too often, mission statements are simply word clouds of generic outcomes. Of course we want our students to be "problem solvers" and "citizens who make a difference." But what do these kinds of general phrases really tell us? We can only wonder what kinds of problems they

FIGURE 7.1

Questions Raised by Coleman's Components of Culture

1. Mission
- Who was involved in creating the mission?
- Is the mission visible in numerous places?
- Do employees, students, and parents know the mission?
- Do all adults try to pursue the mission?

2. Values
- How are new hires oriented?
- What happens at faculty meetings?
- What topics do school handbooks cover?
- Are expectations clear?

3. Practices
- Are students engaged?
- Is there a focus on pedagogy and process?
- What is assessed and reported?
- How is the community kept informed?

4. People
- How are staff hired and fired?
- How are people developed?
- How is teamwork supported?
- How is collegiality among faculty supported?

5. Narrative
- What distinguishes the school?
- Is culture reinforced?
- What stories are told?
- What are the school's traditions?

6. Place
- Is the school clean and safe?
- Is the school inviting?
- What messages are salient?
- Does the school space support learning?

should solve and how they might make a difference. For example, consider the following doubtlessly well-intentioned phrases taken from mission statements that simply do not cast a shadow:

- The X school "exists to provide all students a superior education so that they may achieve their full human potential."
- The Y schools "provide a challenging curriculum that connects students' lives and their future."
- The Z school will "enable all students to become caring, contributing citizens who can succeed in an ever-changing world."

When missions are as broad or as bland as these, they're not meaningful, so we shouldn't be surprised if people in the school aren't familiar with them. Mission statements should do more than offer generalities or list the academic skills that we want to see in our graduates; they should inspire and lead.

Consider the effect on the attitudes and actions of students and staff if mission statements mentioned the Formative Five—empathy, self-control, integrity, embracing diversity, and grit. Such a bold statement would let everyone know that educators are focused on preparing graduates to succeed in the world.

Here are some questions to consider:

Who was involved in creating the mission? Creating or revising a mission statement is a wonderful opportunity for inclusion and a perfect time to reach out to others. Everyone in the school community should be encouraged to offer ideas for consideration. Though the mission statement will ultimately be approved by a small body (presumably the school district's board of directors), this should only happen after a great deal of input from all stakeholders.

Input about the mission can be generated at meetings, either by soliciting individual comments or by having people discuss the mission in small groups. Another way to secure feedback is to ask people to submit ideas on notecards or in a designated space on the school's website. If a mission statement is going be meaningful, it must be shaped by the people who will be bringing it to life. As Hess (2013) says, "Culture, coaching, and inspiration are terrific things. But when staff don't share a common vision, it's tough to build a coherent culture" (p. 135).

Below is the mission statement for New City School. I include it not to suggest that we're perfect, but as an example of a mission that contains specifics that can frame actions. Note that the statement

- Recognizes children's individual strengths.
- States the school's teaching approach ("an integrated Multiple Intelligences curriculum").
- Values joyful learning.
- Prioritizes the personal intelligences ("knowledgeable about themselves and others").
- Emphasizes the importance of diversity.

New City School Mission Statement

New City School develops each child's individual strengths through an integrated Multiple Intelligences curriculum. We prepare children, age 3 through grade 6, to be confident joyful learners who are successful academically, knowledgeable about themselves and others, and who value diversity.

Is the mission statement visible in numerous places? Once established, the mission statement should be pervasive. It should be prominent in entryways to the school and the main hall, visible in the main office, affixed to the cafeteria wall, and posted in classrooms. At New City School, we also included the mission statement on the first page of the Buzz Books and Parent Handbooks that we distributed to families.

Do employees, students, and parents know the mission? If we want everyone to own the mission, we must first ensure that everyone is familiar with it. However, because missions can be long and complex, it may be more realistic to share a slogan that represents the mission statement. For example, at *every* back-to-school night and at *every* parent-education meeting at my school, I have found a way to weave the phrase "academics, the personal intelligences, diversity beyond the numbers, and joyful learning" into my discussions. These terms represent the key points of our mission and are easy to remember and articulate. The bulletin boards outside the main office door are filled student work, photos, and interactive activities that correspond to the four terms.

Misty Johnson, principal of Bissell Elementary School in Twinsburg, Ohio, says that the mission statement of her school is read every day during morning announcements (personal communication, April 13, 2016). This kind of repetition is a powerful way to let everyone, including students, know what is valued.

I also worked to ensure that teachers and administrators used terms related to the school's mission in our communications with parents. When I proofed students' report cards before they were sent home, for example, I might respond to a teacher's draft comment "Jose has focused on working with others" by suggesting that the teacher write "Jose has really worked on his personal intelligences" instead. Likewise, we routinely referred to math skills as "skills in the logical-mathematical intelligence." Regularly using the terms from our mission statement and slogan on important documents like report cards helps promote the mission statement. I also made a point of using the phrases "academic excellence," "personal intelligences," "diversity beyond the numbers," and "joyful learning" in my weekly letters to parents and asked our teachers to do the same.

Do all staff try to pursue the mission? One way to ensure that all staff are actively engaged in achieving the mission is to break them into groups of four or five and ask them to identify how they might teach two of the attributes listed in the mission statement. One of my favorite faculty meetings was one in which I asked our teachers to share what they were doing to generate "joyful learning" in their classrooms. The room was so abuzz with the trading of ideas that it was hard to regain everyone's attention.

Similarly, educators might ask parents how they see the attributes noted in the mission statement manifested in their work or communities or what they do at home to develop the attributes in their children. Working from the mission statement to action steps at least once a year helps to ensure that everyone knows and understands the school's mission.

2: Values

Here are some questions to consider:

How are new hires oriented? We should view the hiring of new employees as opportunities for them to learn both what we do *and* why we do it. It will be particularly important for new employees to understand the rationale for focusing on the Formative Five success skills. In his 2011 book *Start with Why*, Simon Sinek says that leaders of great organizations begin by focusing on *why*. Doing this focuses on purpose and inspires; after that is done, they move to what is done and then how it is accomplished.

It is important to have senior teachers play a significant role in new employee orientations, sharing their experiences, what has worked for them, and what they would do differently. In fact, a good starting point is to ask senior teachers what topics to cover during orientation. All new hires should be taught about the school's mission and culture, not just teachers, and should have the opportunity to hear from current employees who hold the same (or similar) positions.

What happens at faculty meetings? Faculty meetings should really be called *learning meetings* because learning should be their focus. Unfortunately, these meetings are too often a waste of time. Why assemble people just so they can be read to? To make meetings worthwhile, we should apply the same learning principles to adults that we do to students: learners should be active, instruction should be engaging, and a positive tone should be the norm. To this end, teachers should be involved in planning and leading meetings.

For many faculty members, focusing on the Formative Five success skills will be a new and different experience, so meetings should include discussions of the skills, beginning with *why* it is important to teach them. Teachers might share what has worked for them, for example, and even engage in some of the student activities related to the Formative Five. Such experiences will not only improve teachers' understanding and practice, they will also make them more comfortable about leading the same activities in their classrooms.

What topics do school handbooks cover? Often, school handbooks contain little more than legalese and negotiated agreements that delineate how people should behave. Beyond that legally necessary information, handbooks should proclaim what is important in the school's culture. At New City School, our employee handbook includes, in addition to information about sick leave procedures, parent-teacher conferences, and maintenance requests, explanations of the multiple intelligences and notes on faculty collegiality. Sections that speak to the school's culture are also included. Here are two examples:

No Surprises

Although this could go just about anywhere, we're placing it here [near the section on parent-teacher conferences] because often the "no surprises" rule is relevant shortly after a parent-teacher conference! "No surprises" simply means that the administration should not be surprised by something that you know. In other words, if you hear a concern from a parent, or if you've made a mistake in dealing with a kid or a parent (which will happen, none of us are perfect!), let us know as soon as possible. Our jobs are much harder when a parent calls to express a concern and all we can say is, "Gosh, I didn't know about that. I'll have to get back with you." Much better is to inform us so that we can begin working to solve the problem as soon as possible.

Customers vs. Consumers

This is Tom's shorthand way of reminding us that there is a difference between those who "purchase" the service (e.g., by paying tuition in a private school, choosing a home in a particular public school district, or selecting a charter or parochial school) and those who "use" it. The former, the customers, are our kids' parents; the latter, the consumers, are our students. Our efforts must be directed at both.

Our parent handbook, which we distribute to every family at the start of every school year, includes a glossary. In addition to the expected entries (*drop-off and pick-up procedures, field trips, holidays, promptness*), the glossary defines terms that speak to our mission and values (*academics, diversity, joyful learning, multiple intelligences*).

Are expectations clear? Schools or classrooms that focus on the Formative Five skills need to be especially clear about their rules and standards, because focusing on feelings and attitudes can mistakenly convey the impression that any behaviors are permitted. Being upfront about what is acceptable and what is not can avoid misunderstandings and difficulties down the road. It's also important for faculty to understand that our efforts will make a positive difference for students.

As Mankins (2013) notes, "In our experience, too many companies think of culture as a way to make people feel good about where they work and not as a way to help employees—and hence the organization—perform better. High-performing companies think about culture differently. They know that winning cultures aren't just about affiliation; they are also unashamedly about results." Our focus on culture should not get in the way of clarity about what is acceptable.

3: Practices

Practices—the things we do on a day-to-day basis—are what manifest a culture. Lofty goals and a focus on preparing students for success in life are just syllables strung together if the everyday relationships and instruction are lacking. Teachers are the single most important factor in a child's growth after parents, and good teachers will make learning the Formative Five skills interesting and even exciting.

To be fair, it can be challenging for teachers to go beyond traditional instructional goals and focus on the Formative Five skills. Though teaching these skills requires lessons that are more experiential and interactive than usual, designing such lessons can prove to be an enjoyable challenge for teachers, who no doubt would rather be engaged leaders and coaches than script-readers and lesson executioners.

Here are some questions to consider:

Are students engaged? Engagement should be a goal of all instruction. Some very interesting work on the subject is being done by Robert Brisk and his colleagues at the Wellington School in Columbus, Ohio. Their premise is that students become most engaged when they find their work both deeply challenging and highly enjoyable. The teacher's job, then, is to make content meaningful, design interesting lessons, and require students to stretch a bit in learning.

Students at Brisk's school completed surveys to indicate whether they felt challenged by lessons and loved being in a class. Then Brisk and his colleagues plotted the responses on a table like the one in Figure 7.2.

Ideally, all student responses would fall into the "engaged" quadrant at the upper-right, indicating that they feel highly challenged and also love the class. Responses of students who love the class but don't feel challenged belong in the lower-right "entertained" quadrant. Those students who feel challenged by the class but don't enjoy it fall in the

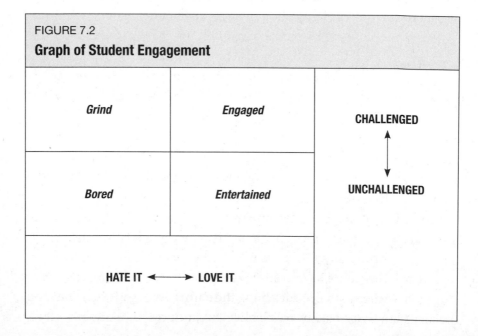

FIGURE 7.2
Graph of Student Engagement

Grind	*Engaged*	**CHALLENGED** ↑
Bored	*Entertained*	↓ **UNCHALLENGED**
HATE IT ←→ LOVE IT		

upper-left "grind" area, and responses from those who neither feel challenged nor enjoy the class fall into the "bored" quadrant on the lower left.

Teachers might use a graph like the one in Figure 7.2 to analyze which students, classes, or subject areas fall where on the "engagement" spectrum. Another idea is to track student engagement over time by conducting the survey at regular intervals. The data from this exercise are a starting point and can be extremely useful in reflecting, questioning, and planning. It would be productive to form a faculty committee for the purpose of determining how best to monitor and facilitate student engagement. (If you would like more information on the project at the Wellington School, contact Robert Brisk at brisk@wellington.org.)

Is there a focus on pedagogy and process? Children learn best when they construct their own understanding, which is likeliest to happen when they are engaged in active learning. I believe that the Formative Five skills are best taught when class discussions and experiential activities are regular features of a classroom. The kinds of lessons that are effective for teaching the Formative Five are not typically found in textbooks or teachers' manuals.

To ensure a focus on pedagogy and process, administrators need to foster a climate of creativity and collegiality among teachers. Barth (1990) lays out four components that, taken together, constitute faculty collegiality:

1. Teachers talking together about students
2. Teachers working together to develop curriculum
3. Teachers observing one another teach
4. Teachers teaching one another

To which I add a fifth component:

5. Teachers and administrators working on learning committees together

Faculty collegiality supports teaching the Formative Five, just as teaching the skills supports faculty collegiality. In teaching the Formative Five, teachers and principals will be planning, learning, and getting out of comfort zones together.

Teachers need to think about times when they can invite people from outside the school—graduates, parents, community members—to discuss the role of Formative Five success skills in their lives. Additionally, teachers might wish to tie a pedagogical goal to the Formative Five (e.g., "I will increase the number of small-group discussions about the Formative Five skills in my classroom and teach students to take the lead in the conversations").

What is assessed and reported? You can tell a lot about a school's culture by looking at its report cards: Is assessment reported solely through grades and check-boxes, or are spaces also provided for teacher narratives? In a classroom or school that focuses on the Formative Five success skills, comments need to be part of students' assessments. This doesn't necessarily mean that they are listed on the report card, but it does mean that progress must be conveyed and shared on a regular basis. (My bias is to include progress in the success skills as part of the report card. Doing so gives a verisimilitude to them.)

At New City School, our report cards are divided according to the multiple intelligences. The first page focuses on the personal intelligences, as we believe they are the most important: assessments of intrapersonal intelligence skills (confidence, motivation, problem solving, responsibility, effort, and work habits) and interpersonal intelligence ones (teamwork and appreciation for diversity). Each area includes a cell for indicating whether the student is having difficulties, progressing toward expectations, meeting expectations, or exceeding expectations. The back of the page is devoted to teachers' narrative comments.

Beginning in 2nd grade, our students participate in the beginning of the first parent-teacher conference of the year to share their academic and personal intelligences goals and how they plan to achieve them. (Typically students then leave the conference so parents and teachers can continue the discussion.) This approach would suit goals related to the Formative Five success skills quite well. For older students particularly, it could be very productive to ask how they think their progress on developing the skills is going. Asking, "How will you know that you've improved?" can elicit deep reflection and discussions.

How is the community informed? All educators benefit when the entire school community knows about the focus on developing Formative Five success skills. Who in the community *wouldn't* want students to leave school with success skills and understandings for positively contributing to society? Though it can be hard to make the time to share what is happening at school with those outside it, the investment helps build support for a Formative Five–focused education.

Of course, our priority should be the internal school community—those who appear in the hallways every weekday. Schools are remarkably insular institutions; communication often doesn't transmit around corners or across roles. For this reason, teachers and principals need to be proactive about informing everyone of what they are doing in the classroom and why. And informing everyone means informing *everyone*: I believe that educators should make time to include administrative and maintenance staff members in occasional faculty meetings and start-of-the-year activities.

4: People

In every school—in every organization, for that matter—it is the people who make the difference. I know this from experience. Over the years I have frequently run into parents of New City School graduates at the grocery store or corner coffee shop, and it was common for them to tell me how much they loved our school. What they really mean by this is that their children had a wonderful teacher, followed by a super teacher, followed by an excellent teacher. It's the quality of the teachers that sets a school apart, and all the more so in schools that focus on the Formative Five.

Here are some questions to consider:

How are staff hired and fired? Hiring is more than simply selecting new employees, although that is critically important. An inclusive hiring process is a great opportunity to build an interviewing team.

Staff members should be actively involved—particularly those who will be working with or in a capacity similar to the new hires—screening resumes and joining in on interviews. If we value teamwork and collegiality, how could we fail to do this?

Once a team is assembled, it is productive for team members to discuss what particular qualities they think the new hires should exhibit. When we reach beyond platitudes ("They will need to like kids, be hard workers, and have the necessary teaching skills"), this question can reveal aspects of the school's mission and values and even tie into the Formative Five skills.

Selecting prospective candidates is always a challenge. It's possible to get a general idea of their skills and knowledge by considering their backgrounds—how and where they were trained and what sorts of experiences they had—by asking them situational questions (e.g., "What do you do when a student _____?"). Getting to the essence of candidates in an interview is considerably more difficult. In one of my *Educational Leadership* columns (Hoerr, 2014), I revealed strong, unique interview questions that I'd solicited from fellow principals. They range from asking candidates to name a book they think faculty should read to asking where "control" sits in the classroom. You can see the article here: www .ascd.org/publications/educational-leadership/feb14/vol71/num05 /What's-Your-Favorite-Interview-Question¢.aspx.

How are people developed? Educators should have access to professional development opportunities to help them achieve their goals. Periodically, principals should touch base with teachers to see how they're progressing and offer to help. In addition, teachers should meet now and then to share their progress on goals and share strategies to help one another succeed. Teachers working on the Formative Five can learn much from others' efforts, regardless of the content area or grade/age of children that their colleagues are teaching.

The most important factor in the development of educators is holding a realistic attitude about growth—recognizing that it is both essential and messy. The phrase "make new mistakes" comes to mind: Painful as they may be, mistakes are part of life, and it's more constructive to learn from them than to avoid them. All of us, adults as well as children, need to get out of our comfort zones and try new things in order to learn, accepting that we're going to make mistakes. I use the phrase "make new mistakes" often with faculty and parents, particularly when I'm sharing my own errors and what I've learned from them. (They are much more frequent than I would like.) A "make new mistakes" attitude supports the development of grit, trust, and risk-taking. According to Duhigg (2016), a study by Google showed that "allowing others to fail without repercussions" (p. 51) was among the strongest predictors of team effectiveness. Figure 7.3 shows the implications of making different types of mistakes.

How is teamwork supported? Teachers need to be able to learn with and from one another, and this is especially true in schools focused on the Formative Five skills. Faculty collegiality is key to growth, and congeniality is a necessary prerequisite. In our too-busy world, we must make time for educators to get to know one another. This isn't as easy as it seems: precisely because we're all so busy, everyone needs reminding that time set aside for collegial interaction is an investment that will ultimately benefit students as well as teachers. (For a vivid example of

---

FIGURE 7.3

Types of Mistakes and Their Implications

Type	Implications	These Mistakes Are ...
Old mistakes	We repeat our errors and do not learn from our experiences.	Dumb
No mistakes	We continue to use the same successful approach. We are error-free, but we aren't learning much.	Not smart
New mistakes	We try new ideas and strategies and learn from our experiences.	Brave and wise

how important this investment is, read Jordan Brenner's 2016 article for *ESPN The Magazine* about NBA basketball team the Golden State Warriors, who routinely eat dinner together on the road because they feel that it makes them a stronger team: "The Warriors' Secret Sauce: Team Dinners on the Road.")

In addition to setting individual goals, all educators should find ways to create team goals with colleagues (e.g., math department goals, 3rd grade teaching goals). Teachers in these teams must reach consensus on strategies to reach their shared goal and sign a document to indicate their commitment. Collaboration—working together as a team—should always be among the strategies. For example, schools might focus on one of the Formative Five skills each year, rotating them on a five-year cycle. Team goals and action plans, signed by everyone on the team, would stem from this schoolwide focus and should be posted in a common area (e.g., teachers' lounge, work room, main office) and periodically revisited at faculty meetings.

How is faculty collegiality supported? Collegiality—adults learning with and from one another—is an essential feature of good schools, but it doesn't happen unless everyone commits to invest the time. The first two of Barth's components of faculty collegiality, teachers talking together about students and teachers working together to develop curriculum, can occur without much difficulty, although focusing on them explicitly helps. However, the third and fourth components, teachers observing one another teach and teachers teaching one another, require intent and tenacity. The component that I added, teachers and administrators working on learning committees together, is a win-win: Administrators can learn much from teachers, and it's always good for teachers to hear administrators' perspectives.

Finally, we need to remember that collegiality is quite different from congeniality. Certainly, we want congenial staff members who ask about one another's families and vacations. But that's just the beginning: What we're really striving for is collegiality, a culture in which people learn with and from one another.

5: Narrative

Mission statements and handbooks are important and necessary, but culture is primarily conveyed through stories, traditions, and artifacts. These are the elements that shout the culture in every organization; the question is whether they develop organically or intentionally.

Here are some questions to consider:

What distinguishes the school? Educators should address this question every year as well as during formal planning, considering what makes their school unique and a source of pride. All schools should strive to improve, and an important part of that is thinking about what sets our school apart from the one across town.

The perceived value of any service, including education, derives from the combination of *relevance* and *differentiation*. This idea was introduced to me by Larry Zarin, formerly the chief marketing officer and senior vice president of Express Scripts. (You can learn more about it here: http://santafe.com/blogs/defining-brand-strength-differentiation-relevance.) Relevance refers to how much consumers (i.e., students and parents) desire the service, and differentiation to how unique the service is. We want our schools to be both relevant (desirable to students and parents) and differentiated (distinct from competing schools). The relationship between relevance, differentiation, and value is shown in Figure 7.4.

Because the Formative Five skills are so necessary yet considered an afterthought in most schools, educators pursuing them have an opportunity to generate enthusiasm for their efforts by ensuring that their school is High Value.

Is culture reinforced? If it's midnight and there's no one in the school, is it still clear what the school culture values? Do decorations in the hallways and classrooms reflect the mission statement? Signs, posters, student work, and even furniture can all reinforce a culture, so we need to be intentional about the messages we give.

What stories are told? The stories we choose to tell and retell can affect perceptions and frame a school's culture. Simply put, if we say

FIGURE 7.4
Relationships among Relevance, Differentiation, and Value

Value = relevance + differentiation

High **RELEVANCE** Low	*COMMODITY* **Desired but neither unique nor different**	*HIGH VALUE* **Differentiated and highly desired**
	OUT OF BUSINESS **Neither desired nor unique**	*GIMCRACK* **Differentiated but not desired**
	Low **DIFFERENTATION** High	

something enough and with enough conviction, the effect is cumulative. To quote Earl Nightingale, "Repetition causes more repetition. Whatever we plant in our subconscious mind and nourish with repetition and emotion will one day become a reality." Author Robert Collier echoes the sentiment when he notes that "constant repetition carries conviction." For example, beginning each faculty meeting by sharing stories of students who have overcome odds reinforces the value of grit. This kind of routine sharing related to Formative Five success skills can also be a part of every parent-education meeting or PTA gathering.

What are the school's traditions? A day or two before the first day of the school year, all New City School staff members receive a t-shirt featuring some sort of unique slogan on it. The shirts are unveiled at a staff meeting after our performing arts teacher plays a special song written for the occasion. The school's name and logo are always evident on the shirt, and the slogan makes a statement about the school's focus for the year. One year, the slogan was *Got Grit*; another year it said *Good Failures*; yet another year, *Multiple Intelligences School*.

Another example of a longstanding tradition at New City School is the awarding of "longevity pins" to staff who have been employed for five years (or any multiple of five). We award the pins every year at our May school picnic, prior to which we solicit positive stories about those receiving the pins from their colleagues to read aloud during the ceremony.

Additional traditions at our school include a Welcome Back Coffee and Donuts event for parents at the start of every year, a Diversity Dinner and Dialogue, and a breakfast where students meet and get to know their pen pals. These traditions show our values. If your school doesn't have these kinds of habits in place, designing them could be a fun and productive task for a school culture committee.

6: Place

The physical environment where we work has a lot to do with our effectiveness and our happiness. We should consider place an opportunity to reinforce culture and to support and highlight the Formative Five success skills.

Questions to consider:

Is the school clean and safe? Everyone in the school community should share the goal of maintaining the cleanliness and safety of the school, students definitely included. This includes, of course, emotional safety—students and staff knowing that they can be themselves without opprobrium. The Formative Five success skills can easily be taught in this context.

Is the school inviting? We want our schools to be settings where everyone feels invited and comfortable, and we need to consciously design them to deliver that message. Are the front doors inviting? Is someone present to welcome visitors and provide security? When people call the school, is the voice on the other end friendly?

Parent-teacher conferences are opportunities to ensure an inviting atmosphere, as they can make everyone anxious at times. If difficulties are being noted, parents may view their children's struggles as reflecting poorly on their parenting and become defensive. Seating for parent conferences should be comfortable (adult seating, not student desks), and that includes seating in the hall where parents await their time to meet. Coffee or water should be provided. These little comforts convey much meaning.

What messages are posted? We want evidence of achievement in the Formative Five skills to be as prominent as evidence of academic achievement. In addition to posting the honor roll where everyone can see it, educators should post lists of students who have displayed empathy, self-control, integrity, embracing diversity, and grit. Posting a separate chart for each of the Formative Five success skills can help to highlight students' progress on them.

Another idea that helps to reinforce a culture of growth is to create a poster titled "Made New Mistakes" that lists examples from students and staff about lessons learned from errors. The dialogue leading to creation of such a poster and the process of creating it help educators to focus on the stories their school tells.

Does space support learning? I believe in "ambient learning." That is, I believe that we learn from experiencing what is around us, even if we are not aware that we are doing so. We should consider halls and walls as spaces to inform and to inspire; they should be filled with the work, presented through both words and pictures, of students who are exhibiting success with the Formative Five skills.

Sadly, the physical spaces of schools and prisons have much in common. They each feature hallways with doors leading to spaces (classrooms and cells) on either side, some common areas for eating, and a focus on timely and quiet passage. To a degree, this makes sense; after all, these buildings are meant to hold hundreds and sometimes thousands of people, so an efficiency and hierarchy is necessary. But focusing too much on institutionalizing the environment can sap inspiration and create an impediment to learning. Cathy Davidson (2011) notes that every element of modern office buildings is "designed to signal that this is not your home; this is not fun; this is not personal; this is not about *you*" (p. 183). This is precisely the type of sterility we want to avoid if our students are to thrive academically and successfully develop the Formative Five.

One aspect of space that educators often overlook is the degree to which it supports collaborative student learning in different-sized groups while also providing room for individual self-reflection. As Cain (2012) notes, "Our lives are shaped as profoundly by personality as by gender or race. And the single most important aspect of personality—the 'north and south of temperament,' as one scientist puts it—is where we fall on the introvert-extrovert spectrum" (p. 2). She continues, "We're told that to be great is to be bold, to be happy is to be sociable. We see ourselves as a nation of extroverts—which means that we've lost sight of who we really are. Depending on which study you consult, one third to one half of Americans are introverts—in other words, *one out of every two or three people you know*" (p. 3). We need to be sure that learning opportunities and physical spaces accommodate both extroverts and introverts.

● ● ●

Culture is the key to our effectiveness and growth. Like the water in which fish live, it is all around us, all of the time; a school's culture affects how we feel, think, and act. Educators must work collaboratively and tenaciously to create a school culture that prepares students for a future in which the only constant will be change.

8

Upon Further Review

If you don't know where you're going, any road will get you there.

—The Cheshire Cat in *Alice's Adventures in Wonderland*

This book is based on the simple premise that the Formative Five skills are very important in preparing students for the real world and can be developed in everyone with focus and effort. But this simple premise has profound implications for how schools operate, how curriculum is developed, how teachers teach, and how principals lead.

A decade ago, focusing on the Formative Five success skills might have seemed outlandish. The priorities of the federal government as expressed in the No Child Left Behind act and, later, the Race to the Top program led a lot of educators to narrowly pursue academic goals. Many teachers and principals have told me that they wished they could focus more on developing students' nonacademic skills, but felt constrained by mandates.

Fortunately, this is beginning to change. The Every Student Succeeds Act of 2015 requires schools to measure at least one nonacademic factor, such as student engagement or grit, in the self-assessments that they report to the government. I find it very encouraging that politicians are catching up with what teachers and principals have known for a long time about what children need. This is captured well in the introduction to *Preparing Youth to Thrive* (Smith et al., 2016), a field book for providing intentional social and emotional skill development:

> Not long ago, success in school meant success in life. We also believed that things like grit and determination were traits people were born with, not skills that could be developed over time. Over the past few decades, hard and soft sciences have produced an impressive body of evidence that teaches us two very new, very important things. First, that we can take our innate abilities and cultivate them, just like we build up muscle, dexterity, and language fluency. And secondly, that social and emotional skills matter just as much in determining life satisfaction and success as traditional intelligence. The use of the word 'skills' here is intentional. These qualities are not only innate. They can be taught. And, they can be learned. (p. v)

In this chapter, I will address three points that may help teachers and principals bring the Formative Five success skills to life: related constructs; assessment; and relationships.

Related Constructs

Here are a few models of thinking and learning that support teaching the Formative Five:

Multiple intelligences (MI). In his classic book *Frames of Mind* (1983), Howard Gardner identifies seven kinds of intelligences (later eight). Two of these, intrapersonal intelligence and interpersonal intelligence, focus directly on how we think about ourselves and others. Simply put, intrapersonal intelligence is self-knowledge, and interpersonal intelligence is the knowledge of others. Gardner recognized that these categories qualified as intelligences because they could be used to solve problems.

Emotional intelligence. In *Emotional Intelligence* (1995), Daniel Goleman further cites self-management (i.e., the Formative Five skill of self-control) as a critical aspect of emotional intelligence.

Habits of mind. Art Costa's habits of mind framework (Costa & Kallick, 2008) includes 16 components, a few of which directly correspond to the Formative Five skills: persisting (grit), managing impulsivity (self-control), and listening with understanding and empathy (empathy).

Executive function. According to Cooper-Kahn and Dietzel (2008), executive function is "a set of processes that all have to do with managing oneself and one's resources in order to achieve a goal. It is an umbrella term for the neurologically-based skills involving mental control and self-regulation" (p. 9).

Distributed intelligence (DI). This is the ability to draw from the resources around us (e.g., tools, symbols, portfolios, forms, calculators, computers, and not least individuals) in order to solve problems. A strong DI stems from a high intrapersonal intelligence that enables one to tap into the talents of others. To quote Steve Jobs, "Great things in business are never done by one person. They're done by a team of people." That's certainly true in schools, too!

Too often we view problem solving as a solitary responsibility, when in reality most complex problems are solved through teamwork and collaboration. Helping students understand that working together is a form of DI reinforces the idea that it is an important lifelong skill. (In talking about DI with older students, teachers might refer to James Surowiecki's 2004 book *The Wisdom of Crowds,* which maintains that groups are often smarter than any one individual within them and are better at decision making than individuals are.)

The relationships between each of the above-mentioned constructs and the Formative Five skills are depicted in Figure 8.1. What all five models share is a focus on student reflection and collaboration. Students need to analyze situations and consider their biases and skills when determining how to engage in problem solving.

Assessing Formative Five Skills

We need to know that our efforts to embed the Formative Five in students' minds (and, yes, hearts) are effective. In fact, the federal government's

FIGURE 8.1

Relationships Among Learning Constructs and the Formative Five Skills

Formative Five Skills	Multiple Intelli- gences	Emotional Intelli- gence	Habits of Mind	Executive Function	Distributed Intelli- gence
Empathy	X	X	X		
Self-Control	X	X	X	X	X
Integrity	X	X			
Embracing Diversity	X	X			X
Grit	X	X	X	X	

new thrust, the Every Student Succeeds Act (ESSA), requires states to measure at least one nonacademic factor, and that will require some sort of assessment. But this is not easy to do; rather, it's not easy to do well and to do with validity. That's because the measure of these attitudes and skills is best demonstrated daily by students' myriad behaviors in complex interactions and situations, not by their multiple-choice test responses. Standardized tests are inadequate for determining students' progress in success skills, and yet it will be very tempting to rely on them.

Kate Zernike notes the tensions surrounding measuring social-emotional skills in an article, "Testing for Joy and Grit." In it, Angela Duckworth expresses opposition to using standardized measures to assess progress on grit, saying "I do not think we should be doing this; it is a bad idea" (Zernike, 2016). In *Helping Children Succeed* (2016), Paul Tough recognizes this difficulty but also understands the need to evaluate: "If you can't clearly identify and measure skills, it's hard to convince people to take them seriously," he says (p. 67). Clearly, we need to assess students on these attitudes and skills to ensure that kids are growing, to gain feedback on our efforts, and to inform the community about our successes. The question is "how?"

The best way to assess progress in the Formative Five (as well as in any other non-academic area) is with intentionality and by observation and reflection.

Intentionality. Simply put, we—students and teachers—formally state our intention to improve in these areas and focus on how we can determine growth. This requires us to have a baseline (improvement from what?) and gives verisimilitude to our efforts. As the Formative Five success skills are explained and their importance is appreciated (see suggestions at the end of each of the chapters), students should begin by assessing how they see their proficiency in each area. Self-reporting has its limitations, but it is an appropriate way to begin.

Observation. Teachers need to be sharp observers of their students throughout the day because often growth in a Formative Five success skill occurs when there is less teacher direction and control. In fact, this kind of pedagogy supports teaching the Formative Five. As Paul Tough (2016) notes, in describing a "deeper learning" (p. 104), in student-centered schools—as classrooms are likely to become when the Formative Five are embraced—there will be more inquiry-based instruction:

> [This] means that in the classroom, teachers tend to engage students in discussions rather than just lecturing to them; project-based learning, in which groups of students spend much of their time working, often in groups, on elaborate projects that might take weeks or months to complete; and performance-based assessments, in which student are judged not primarily by the scores on end-of-semester exams, but by the portfolios, presentations, artwork, and written work they produce throughout the year. (p. 105)

These kinds of student interactions and activities can offer rich insights into students' Formative Five attitudes and skills.

The students' self-reports and progress can also be measured through rubrics. Teachers can create a rubric for each of the Formative Five (as is shown for grit in Figure 6.2) or, even better, they can facilitate a class discussion in developing them. Student input always leads to a more relevant and meaningful product. Students can then refer to a posted rubric throughout the year or after they have engaged in a discussion or activity that is particularly germane to a specific skill. They could, for example, use the rubric numbers as a short-hand way of assessing the empathy, integrity, or embracing of diversity shown by a character in literature. Teachers could ask students to reflect on their self-control or grit after they have been involved in a difficulty.

Student status and progress on the Formative Five should be shared with parents. This might be done by asking students to discuss an activity and their role in it during an evening discussion, or it could happen through students sharing drawings or songs. Giving students an opportunity to use their stronger intelligences increases their enthusiasm and ability to share. Presentations and performances that include stories, reflections, and a range of intelligences will not be as quantifiable as a standardized test, and that's fine. Particularly with the Formative Five, it is better to value validity—how can students show what they have learned?—than pursue reliability, seeking quantifiable and reproducible data.

Students' progress should be incorporated into formal reports, which should periodically be shared with parents as attachments to formal reports or incorporated into the reports. Assessments should be done *with* students, not *to* them; students should be actively involved in helping to plan how their progress is measured and what the next steps should be. We never want to embarrass a student, and the potential for this to occur may be higher with the Formative Five. Teachers and students should work together to focus on trajectory, progress, and what is shared to be sure that no student is put at risk.

Reflection. Reflection—stepping back to consider your thoughts and actions and how you might learn from them—is an integral part of growth. The importance of reflection as integral to learning is true whether hitting a baseball or maintaining a relationship. Individuals who have a strong intrapersonal intelligence do this by nature; most of us are not so lucky. Teachers need to allocate time for students to learn from their experiences by reflecting, sometimes individually and occasionally as a group (although always beginning in private thought), and sharing. That sharing might be internal, writing in a journal or picking a rubric number, it might be to the class, or it could be with a teacher, either in person or by a note. Too often students do not learn from their mistakes without taking time to reflect.

The Importance of Relationships

Establishing positive relationships—between teachers and students, between administrators and teachers, and among teachers, principals, and students' parents—is the key to successfully teaching the Formative Five success skills. That's especially the case because these areas require all of us to venture out of our comfort zones; we need to know what is expected and that others can be trusted.

Teachers and students. In doing research for this book, I've read numerous books and articles about each success skill; I've read books and articles on leadership; I've interviewed scores of principals, teachers, and parents; I've talked with students; and I've exchanged e-mails with educators from around the world. People's priorities vary, and their approaches to education and learning are often influenced by the role they play. The one constant, however, is that relationships matter. Our students must understand that we know them and care for them. Maya Angelou said it best: "I've learned that people will forget what you said, people will forget what you did, but people will never forget how you made them feel." I know this to be true. Mrs. Mayfield, my 1st grade teacher many years ago, gave me the care that placed me on a trajectory that changed my life, and I have never forgotten her.

Paul Tough (2016) says,

> When kids feel a sense of belonging at school, when they receive the right kind of messages from an adult who believes they can succeed and who is attending to them with some degree of compassion and respect, they are more likely to show up to class, to persevere longer at difficult tasks, and to deal more resiliently with the countless small-scale setbacks and frustrations that make up the typical student's school day. (p. 73)

Sadly, this focus on relationships is an example of common sense that isn't all that common. In too many schools and classrooms the focus is on academics only. Teachers are unable to get to know students personally. Too often, school schedules, and sometimes school norms, don't allow teachers and students to share who they are as people. It's hard to feel that the teacher is your advocate if you don't feel that the teacher knows you. While these descriptions are not the norm, they occur in too many schools.

In contrast, educators who teach the Formative Five will take the time to know their students. They will appreciate that the time spent listening to students talk about their weekend, share their worries, and talk about their hopes is an investment. When students understand that they are known and cared for, they can better handle difficulties and are more likely to venture out of their comfort zones.

Administrators and teachers. To successfully teach the Formative Five success skills, teachers and principals must work as colleagues. Educators who embrace this new direction will find themselves discussing both their own and their students' growth with one another, bringing them closer together.

In the same sense that students need to feel cared for and known, so, too, do teachers. Teachers must know that principals want to help them succeed and understand that mistakes are part of the process. And they need to know that principals value them as people. That is especially the case when they are pursuing a new area, such as the Formative Five. It is hard for teachers to see a principal as an advocate if the principal hasn't taken the time to know them as persons.

Years ago, as a first-year principal, I made the mistake of not regularly inquiring about the health of one of my teachers' spouse, who was stricken with cancer. I now see that I was uncomfortable raising the issue, so I simply didn't do so. I was friendly to her and we talked about curriculum and instruction, but I was also aware that we had not really connected. During a meeting at the end of the year, she told me how hurt she was that I never asked about her husband, and she said that it was more difficult for her to trust me because I didn't seem to value her as a person. As you might imagine, I felt terrible and apologized pro-fusely, and it's a lesson that I have never forgotten.

Likewise, teachers need to make the effort to get to know their prin-cipals and let them know that advocacy works both ways. Once a teacher was telling me about her need for positive feedback, and I shared that this was true for me, too. Often, I told her, I do something that is helpful to you but I never hear about it. Her eyes widened. "I don't need to do that," she said quickly, "you're an administrator!"

In a good school, everyone tries to support one another. In a great school, everyone makes the time for this to happen.

Among teachers, principals, and students' parents. For the par-ents of most students, having children who are learning the Formative Five will be a new experience. While they may endorse this thrust—who could be against empathy or integrity?—parents will naturally have questions. *How is this being taught? What is being ignored because of this focus?* And possibly, *Will my parenting skills be criticized?*

In discussing preschool programs that focus on noncognitive growth, Heckman (2013) notes: "Many successful programs change the values and motivations of the child. Some of these may run counter to the values of certain parents" (p. 37). Although I might quibble with the word *counter* in the case of Formative Five, it is true that teaching them can offer students experiences quite different from those that their parents had. Our job as school leaders is to help them reach a level of comfort with the new way of doing things; to quote Max DePree, "the first job of a leader is to define reality" (1990, p. 11).

Teachers and principals will need to be sure to communicate often and openly about what they are doing and why they are doing it. Fol-lowing Simon Sinek's advice, each year should begin with an explana-tion of why teaching the Formative Five will play an important role in the school. Once the why is established, once parents see how their chil-dren's chances for success will be improved because of this emphasis, then they are ready to learn how the school will accomplish this. Weekly newsletters and parent education evenings should certainly mention and occasionally focus on the Formative Five. Juxtaposed quotes from famous people and current students about the value of these attributes can be quite powerful.

The fact that the Formative Five skills don't yield percentiles or letter grades can reinforce parents' skepticism. For this reason, it is important to proactively help parents understand the difference between success in school and success in life. Here are some articles that may be good starting points for discussion:

- "What's Worth Learning in School?" (2015), by Lory Hough. *Harvard Ed.* Available: www.gse.harvard.edu/news/ed/15/01/whats-worth-learning-school

- "What IQ Tests Really Measure" (2011), by Farnam Street. *Business Insider.* Available: www.businessinsider.com/what-iq-tests-really-measure-2011-5

- "Data That Count" (2008/2009), by Thomas Hoerr. *Educational Leadership.* Available: www.ascd.org/publications/educational-leadership/dec08/vol66/num04/Data-That-Count.aspx

- "How Smart Should a President Be?" (2015), by David Z. Hambrick. *Scientific American.* Available: www.scientificamerican.com/article/how-smart-should-the-president-be/

- "Why Parents Need to Let Their Children Fail" (2013), by Jessica Lahey. *The Atlantic.* Available: www.theatlantic.com/national/archive/2013/01/why-parents-need-to-let-their-children-fail/272603/

- "Is There School Today?" (2015), by Philip Kovacs. *Huffington Post.* Available: www.huffingtonpost.com/philip-kovacs/is-there-school-today_b_6712590.html

- "Is the Drive for Success Making Our Children Sick?" (2016), by Vicki Abeles. *New York Times.* Available: www.nytimes.com/2016/01/03/opinion/sunday/is-the-drive-for-success-making-our-children-sick.html

Consider sharing these articles with parents, either as supplemental information or as the basis for discussion on a parent-education evening.

Every educator should view the school's halls and walls as learning spaces; they present opportunities for displays of student work that evince the curriculum focus. Everyone who enters the school—students, parents, caregivers, staff members, other educators, and the delivery man—should come away feeling informed and enthusiastic about the school's mission and work.

Finally, regardless of role, the best relationships feature two-way communication.

I routinely solicit feedback from families during the year, including through a Spring Parent Survey. In it, I ask parents to write down the grade level of their student; which of our school's four pillars—academics, the personal intelligences, diversity beyond the numbers, and joyful learning—they consider most important; whether I was friendly and helpful in our interactions; whether their parent-teacher conferences were productive; and whether their child's individual needs had been met. As you might imagine, the feedback was always informative (even if sometimes hard to hear). Educators are very good at talking to and explaining, and we need to be better at asking and listening.

Let's Not Forget Happiness

The word *happy* is not used very often in this book, which is both understandable and a bit sad. It's understandable because the word itself is rarely found in mission statements, on standardized tests, as part of a scope and sequence, or even at faculty meetings. It's sad, of course, because we all want to be happy. Fortunately, developing the Formative Five will lead to happiness: students who are more in control of their emotions, more productive in their efforts, and more accepting and appreciative of others will certainly find greater joy in life than those who lack these attributes.

As we think about developing the Formative Five skills in students, we should also think about orienting our students to focus on their strengths and relish their successes. We want them to bring an optimistic lens to new situations. As Sean Achor says in his TED talk, "The Happy Secret to Better Work" (2011):

Every time your brain has a success, you just changed the goalpost of what success looked like. You got good grades, now you have to get better grades, you got into a good school and after you get into a better one, you got a good job, now you have to get a better job, you hit your sales target, we're going to change it. And if happiness is on the opposite side of success, your brain never gets there. We've pushed happiness over the cognitive horizon, as a society. And that's because we think we have to be successful, then we'll be happier.

Achor says that if we are happy, we are more likely to achieve our goals. He recommends getting in the habit of journaling our successes and of consciously executing random acts of kindness (which, of course, wouldn't be so random after all). High aspirations are important, but we also need to help our students (and ourselves) appreciate the successes. Because working on the Formative Five skills may be new and difficult, this is particularly crucial.

It Worked for Me

In many respects, the experiences that I share in this book are simply common sense lessons that are familiar to educators everywhere. That said, it isn't always easy to implement these ideas. Believe me, I know: far more often than I would have liked, I reflected on my actions and vowed to do things differently—and occasionally, I actually did!

One thing I do know is that sometimes leaders, myself included, fail to remember that adults are simply older children. That is, the same principles apply to their learning as to students. Adults and children both learn best when the learning is developmental (addressing their ability and readiness to learn), when the learning is interesting and experiential, and when they know that the teacher or leader understands and appreciates them. (The old adage "They won't care what you know until they know that you care" applies here.)

To this end, principals need to invest time in truly getting to know their teachers. Leadership is based on relationships, and developing relationships takes time and energy. As Fullan (2014) says, "To increase impact, principals should use their time differently. They should direct their energies to developing the group" (p. 55). He further notes that the most effective principals are "those who [define] their roles as facilitators of teacher success rather than instructional leaders" (p. 73).

I've spent much of my time as a school leader encouraging and developing teacher growth through collegiality, which appears as an item on all my teachers' summative evaluations. One good barometer of collegiality can be found in faculty meetings. In a truly collegial school culture, faculty meetings should focus on teacher learning; they are times for everyone to gain new skills or knowledge. I strongly believe that we should create settings where our teachers learn and smile at as they do so.

Thank you for your interest and your time. I hope that my ideas have been helpful, and I would be delighted to hear from you. Good luck on your Formative Five journey!

Tom Hoerr

Appendix A:
Self-Assessment Surveys

Student Self-Assessment Survey: Empathy

Note: This survey is designed to stimulate reflection and discussion. It will not be counted for a grade.

Directions: Place a 1 (strongly disagree), 2 (disagree), 3 (not sure), 4 (agree), or 5 (strongly agree) after each item.

1. As long as everyone gets what they want, everyone will be happy. ___

2. People can view things differently and still be kind and caring. ___

3. I can't learn much from people who are different from me. ___

4. When people disagree with me, I ask them why they feel that way. ___

5. I only enjoy hanging around people like me. ___

6. People who are different can have much more in common than it might seem at first. ___

7. If people who see things differently than me knew what I know, they would see things the same way that I do. ___

8. It is important for everyone's voice to be heard. ___

9. I try to figure what others want in a relationship with me. ___

10. If you are right, others will be eager to join you. ___

Scoring:

___ (A) Total points for 2, 4, 6, 8, 9

___ (B) Total points for 1, 3, 5, 7, 10

___ (C) Subtract (B) from (A) for your "empathy" score

If you scored

- *18 or higher:* You understand empathy.
- *14–17:* You should give a bit more thought to issues of empathy.
- *13 or lower:* You and your teacher should have a conversation about empathy.

Student Self-Assessment Survey: Self-Control

Note: This survey is designed to stimulate reflection and discussion. It will not be counted for a grade.

Directions: Place a 1 (strongly disagree), 2 (disagree), 3 (not sure), 4 (agree), or 5 (strongly agree) after each item.

1. I can improve my self-control in school situations. ___

2. It is better to be creative than to have self-control. ___

3. Having strong self-control means that you will always be successful. ___

4. I can improve my self-control in situations outside of school. ___

5. Using self-control always means resisting something fun. ___

6. If you are good at something, you won't need much self-control. ___

7. Before a challenging situation, it is helpful to anticipate why it might be hard to manage self-control. ___

8. After a challenging situation, it is important to reflect on what made it hard to maintain self-control. ___

9. We naturally have self-control in areas at which we excel. ___

10. Improving my self-control in one area can help it improve in other areas. ___

Scoring:

___ (A) Total points for 1, 4, 7, 8, 10

___ (B) Total points for 2, 3, 5, 6, 9

___ (C) Subtract (B) from (A) for your "self-control" score

If you scored

- *18 or higher:* You understand self-control.
- *14–17:* You should give a bit more thought to issues of self-control.
- *13 or lower:* You and your teacher should have a conversation about self-control.

Student Self-Assessment Survey: Integrity

Note: This survey is designed to stimulate reflection and discussion. It will not be counted for a grade.

Directions: Place a 1 (strongly disagree), 2 (disagree), 3 (not sure), 4 (agree), or 5 (strongly agree) after each item.

1. There are times when it is OK to be less than honest. ___

2. If I am not sure what is right or wrong, there is a family member or educator I can talk to. ___

3. It's important for me to be honest even if other people don't know I am. ___

4. It's most important for me to be honest when money is involved. ___

5. Everyone deserves to be treated in an honest way. ___

6. As long as I am being honest, it is not important for others to know how I think. ___

7. As long as you believe something, it doesn't matter whether you show it and others know it. ___

8. If someone else is being dishonest or unfair, I should let them know. ___

9. Being honest may mean saying something that costs me. ___

10. It is important that my friends know that I agree with them. ___

Scoring:

___ (A) Total points for 2, 3, 5, 8, 9

___ (B) Total points for 1, 4, 6, 7, 10

___ (C) Subtract (B) from (A) for your "integrity" score

If you scored

- *18 or higher:* You understand integrity.

- *14–17:* You should give a bit more thought to issues of integrity.

- *13 or lower:* You and your teacher should have a conversation about integrity.

Student Self-Assessment Survey: Embracing Diversity

Note: *This survey is designed to stimulate reflection and discussion. It will not be counted for a grade.*

Directions: Place a 1 (strongly disagree), 2 (disagree), 3 (not sure), 4 (agree), or 5 (strongly agree) after each item.

1. Every student comes to school with the same chances for success. ___

2. I have close friends of different races, ethnicities, and genders. ___

3. Everyone would get along better if we all knew more about my culture. ___

4. I respect the holidays and celebrations of religions and groups that are different than mine. ___

5. I consciously reach out to students who are in a minority group (racial, religious, sexual orientation, etc.). ___

6. The election of President Obama means that racial bias is no longer a problem in the United States. ___

7. I am comfortable being around people regardless of their sexual orientation. ___

8. Boys are naturally better athletes and leaders than girls. ___

9. It's OK to use stereotypical language as long as you're just kidding. ___

10. I understand that society has favored some groups over others. ___

Scoring:

___ (A) Total points for 2, 4, 5, 7, 10

___ (B) Total points for 1, 3, 6, 8, 9

___ (C) Subtract (B) from (A) for your "embracing diversity" score

If you scored

- *18 or higher:* You understand embracing diversity.
- *14–17:* You should give a bit more thought to issues of embracing diversity.
- *13 or lower:* You and your teacher should have a conversation about embracing diversity.

Student Self-Assessment Survey: Grit

Note: This survey is designed to stimulate reflection and discussion. It will not be counted for a grade.

Directions: Place a 1 (strongly disagree), 2 (disagree), 3 (not sure), 4 (agree), or 5 (strongly agree) after each item.

1. No matter how difficult a task is, I keep trying. ___

2. I would rather practice something I do well than try to learn something new. ___

3. I am often distracted when things are hard. ___

4. Learning in school should be easy. ___

5. I usually work harder than my classmates. ___

6. It is important to me that I don't make mistakes. ___

7. I would rather get a B in a new area of learning than an A in an area I'm already good at studying. ___

8. Learning needs to be fun. ___

9. It's OK if I make a mistake or two while learning. ___

10. If something is difficult, I am sure to devote extra time to it. ___

Scoring:

___ (A) Total points for 1, 5, 7, 9, 10

___ (B) Total points for 2, 3, 4, 6, 8

___ (C) Subtract (B) from (A) for your "grit" score

If you scored

- *18 or higher:* You understand grit.
- *14–17:* You should give a bit more thought to issues of grit.
- *13 or lower:* You and your teacher should have a conversation about grit.

Appendix B:
Family Letters

It's important for parents to know not only *what* is happening in classrooms but also *why*. So I sent a letter to families every week during the school year and used it to share logistical information and update them on our activities.

February 27, 2015

Hi there, everyone!

Here's a really great article from Empathy Educates, "Is There School Today?" Sadly, it captures the educational reality for a lot of kids. Check Not Joyful Learning or paste the following link into your browser: http://empathyeducates.org/is-there-school-today. I'd love for you to take a few minutes to read it and share your thoughts with me.

From Laurie: For the eighth consecutive year, all 4th, 5th, and 6th grade students participated in the New City Geography Bee. The students compete in teams first in their classrooms or social studies block, and then in a schoolwide bee. The teams work together to answer a series of questions that get progressively more difficult.

No School

Parent-Teacher Conferences are held next week, so there is NO SCHOOL on Friday, March 6.

Our two-week spring break begins on Monday, March 16, and we return to school on Monday, March 30.

The Police Were Here!

From Mary, Assistant Head for Student and Family Support: The difficulties in Ferguson (and elsewhere) have caused people to sometimes question the role of the police. They are here to serve and protect, yet that is not always how they are portrayed. To reinforce that the police are on our side, we asked representatives of the St. Louis Police Department to come and talk to our students.

Last week, three officers came to talk with the 5th and 6th graders about their jobs and place in the community and to answer questions. The 5th and 6th graders asked about the officers' impressions of the events in Ferguson as well as several other topics. The officers were very good at relating to our students and were very impressed with the thoughtful and informed exchange.

The officers will return to talk to students in other grades as well. We are hoping to have an ongoing relationship with them, and this was a really good start.

Join Us: A Discussion of For the Sake of All

From Stephanie, Director of Diversity: Did you know that in St. Louis . . .

- The rates of unemployment among African Americans are almost four times those of whites.
- Fifty-seven percent of African Americans in St. Louis attain some college education, compared with 74 percent of whites.
- The high number of deaths due to poverty and low levels of education has a large economic cost for the St. Louis region, with the impact estimated at $7.8 billion.

We all pay a price when people in our region lack economic and educational opportunities. Please join us for a discussion on the For the

Sake of All project. Please join us for a thoughtful and engaging discussion on Tuesday, March 3, from 5:30 to 6:30 p.m.

Free child care is available for all New City School students. Please RSVP to Stephanie if you plan to attend (and indicate if you require child care) or if you have any questions.

DODGED, DUCKED, and DOVE for Financial Aid

From Jessica, Director of Advancement: Thank you to the dodgeballers who came out and played in the friendly New City dodgeball tournament this past Saturday night. The proceeds went to our financial aid program. Fun was had by all!

Keeping Up With Technology

From Liz, our technology specialist: Parents often ask Scott and me how we "keep up with technology," especially regarding safety of kids. We'd like to share a few resources that we rely on to keep us updated.

I currently use the app Zite (iOS and Android) to get most of my information, favoring topics that are geared towards parenting, safety and media issues, and trends with children and technology. Zite aggregates articles from news sources and blogs based on your reading trends and favored terms, so you don't have to go searching aimlessly for resources. (If you've ever used Flipboard, you'll recognize Zite as a similar app.) Terms I have favored include social media, education, iOS apps, internet safety, and websites such as Common Sense Media. Generally, with these topics favored, issues and news I need to know about as a technology specialist will appear in my feed.

We also participate in the "tech world" and heavily recommend joining the apps and social media services your children are using. This list will help you get started. Note the "what parents need to know" section of each service.

Lastly, Common Sense Media is a great resource for parents who are interested in reviews and parent concerns of websites, games, and social media services. It's probably the most on-top-of-it resource currently available for parents looking to review technology.

Sign Up for Movie Day!
Don't forget to sign up for Movie Day! Join us on Sunday, March 1, at noon, for a special showing of 'Babe'! Moviegoers will enjoy the film, a drink, and snack in the setting of MX Movies, located in downtown's historic Mercantile Exchange building. Children must be accompanied by an adult. Adults may either watch the movie or hang out in the lounge with access to beverages for purchase. Tickets for the movie are $15. A drink and a snack are included with ticket purchase.

Use the sign-up sheet in the hallway at New City! See you there!

Safety, please!
Please be extra sure to drive safely when you're around New City School. That includes:

- Only dropping off and picking up kids when their door is on the curbside.
- Only dropping off and picking up kids at intersections.
- Coming to a full stop at Waterman and Westminster.
- Driving s-l-o-w-l-y. We have lots of little legs outside.

And please remember that Westminster Avenue, the street to our north, is a private street and cannot be used for parking.

Thank you!

Is Grit Racist?
"Is Grit Racist?" is a pretty silly question in my mind. Yet that was the headline of an article in a recent issue of *Education Week:* http://blogs.edweek.org/edweek/DigitalEducation/2015/01/is_grit_racist.html

Here's my letter to the editor (just published): www.edweek.org/ew/articles/2015/02/18/grit-helps-everyone-gain-real-world-success.html. Reactions are welcome!

Thomas R. Hoerr, PhD
Head of School
trhoerr@newcityschool.org

March 6, 2015

Yo, how's it going?

We have NO SCHOOL on Friday, March 6, due to Parent-Teacher Conferences. In next week's FL, I'll ask you about your conferences.

This weekly FL and the weekly PL sent by classroom teachers play an important role in your child's educational experience. The letters contain information about what's happening in the classroom, what's going on at school, as well as educational ideas and questions. But everyone's inbox is already filled to the brim, I know. WHEN would you like to get your child's weekly class PL? We're wondering if there's a better day/time than on Fridays at 6 p.m.

Also, what about my weekly FL? I sent last week's FL on Wednesday night; was that better? Do you have any preferences on when it comes? Any suggestions for content (other than better jokes?)?

Spring Breaaaaaak!

Our last day of school before Spring Break is Friday, March 13. We are off for two weeks, resuming on Monday, April 30.

From Shannah, art/spatial teacher: In 3rd grade art, we looked at images of Native Americans in various formats; fine art, posters, cartoons, and sports. We examined how these images of Native Americans influence our perceptions, and we questioned who should have control of these images and why.

Our Winning Equations Team

On Tuesday, February 24, 10 of our 5th graders participated in Gifted Resource Council's Academic Challenge Cup for Equations at UMSL. More than 1,400 students from more than 80 public, private, and parochial schools in the St. Louis metropolitan area participated in this competition over a seven-day period in February and March. The competition consisted of a series of half-day events designed to challenge students in grades 2 through 8 in mathematics, language usage, and creative problem solving.

Movie Night Is March 6
From Jessica: Our Social Action Committee will be showing two movies on Friday, March 6, at 6:30 p.m. (doors open at 6:00), one in the theater and one in the library. This way we hope to reach all age ranges! We will be watching *STAR WARS* (the original) and *THE LEGO MOVIE*!

This is a family event, and children must be accompanied by an adult, but you may choose to split up and watch different movies! For example, if one parent comes with two kids, the parent may watch a movie with one while the other child watches the other movie in a different location. You are welcome to invite families outside of the New City community as well! We are asking for $5 per person donations for movie tickets and will have some snacks available for purchase. No RSVP necessary! Just show up and join us in the fun!

Writing About Ferguson
In addition to educating our students and preparing them for success in life—not settling for success in school—New City also plays a leadership role in the larger educational community. That's true educationally—we were the second school to implement MI and are now the leader in MI—as well as with our focus on diversity. A recent example is that Stephanie, our Director of Diversity and a 5th grade teacher, wrote an article for *Educational Leadership* that described some of the ways in which our faculty and students were responding to the difficulties in Ferguson. You can see Stephanie's article here: www.ascd.org /publications/educational-leadership/mar15/vol72/num06/Teaching -%C2%A3Ferguson%C2%A3.aspx.

I also used our response to the killing of Michael Brown and the subsequent community disruption in Ferguson as the topic for my monthly "Principal Connection" column. You can see it here: www.ascd.org /publications/educational-leadership/mar15/vol72/num06/Responding -to-Ferguson.aspx

Stephanie and I would welcome any thoughts that you have about these articles (or diversity at New City School).

The World Is in SO Much Better Shape. Really!

It's easy to look around and see all the negative things, things that aren't as good as we'd like, times and places where progress hasn't occurred as quickly as we hoped, and where problems are still unsolved. That's true, from Ferguson to the state of public education in many places, to the high percentage of children living in poverty, both in the United States and the world. Clearly, we have a long way to go.

That said, things have improved quite a bit. It may be hard to recognize it when you're in the middle of things, but it's true! There are data—on hunger, mortality, disease, crime, and so on—that show just how far the world has come, even though we probably don't realize it. Check out the graphs. I'd love to hear your reactions!

Is Grit Racist? Again

Our focus on grit falls within our valuing the personal intelligences. My comment "Who you are is more important than what you know" is a way to convey that success in the world, however you define it, depends upon far more than academic skills. Successful adults know how to work with others, they are good teammates, they care about people, they respect and appreciate others regardless of demographic variable, and they show grit! Those are the kinds of things on which we work each and every day.

Looking way ahead, we will be hosting our second PETER MARTIN CONCERT here on Friday evening, May 22. The New City School jazz band will also perform. Last year's concert was spectacular, and you won't want to miss this one!

Thomas R. Hoerr, PhD
Head of School
trhoerr@newcityschool.org

References

Abeles, V. (2016, January 2). Is the drive for success making our children sick? *New York Times.* Retrieved from http://www.nytimes.com/2016/01/03/opinion /sunday/is-the-drive-for-success-making-our-children-sick.html

Achor, S. (2011, May). *The happy secret to better work* [Video]. Available: http://www .ted.com/talks/shawn_achor_the_happy_secret_to_better_work?language=en

Ad Council. (2015, March 5). *Love has no labels* [Video]. Available: https://www .youtube.com/watch?v=PnDgZuGIhHs

Alexie, S. (2007). *The absolutely true diary of a part-time Indian.* New York: Little, Brown.

Angelica, A. D. (2016, March 15). Will this new "socially assistive robot" from MIT Media Lab (or its progeny) replace teachers? *Kurzweil Accelerating Intelligence.* Retrieved from http://www.kurzweilai.net/will-this-new-socially-assistive -robot-from-mit-media-lab-or-its-progeny-replace-teachers

Angier, N. (2013, November 26). The changing American family. *New York Times Magazine.* Retrieved from http://www.nytimes.com/2013/11/26/health /families.html

Associated Press. (2015, October 24). Obama calls for capping class time devoted to standardized tests. Retrieved from http://www.pbs.org/newshour/rundown /obama-calls-cap-class-time-devoted-standardized-tests/

Balson, R. (1990). *Once we were brothers.* New York: St. Martin's Press.

Barth, R. S. (1990). *Improving schools from within: Teachers, parents, and principals can make the difference.* San Francisco: Jossey-Bass.

BBC. (2012, March 14). *Crossing a St. Louis street that divides communities* [Video]. Available: http://www.bbc.com/news/magazine-17361995

Beals, M. (1994). *Warriors don't cry: A searing memoir of the battle to integrate Arkansas' Little Rock High.* New York: Pocket Books.

Boehm, C. (2012). *Moral origins: The evolution of virtue, altruism, and shame.* New York: Basic Books.

Boyle, T. C. (1995). *The tortilla curtain.* New York: Penguin.

Brenner, J. (2016, April 10). The Warriors' secret sauce: Team dinners on the road. *ESPN The Magazine.* Retrieved from http://espn.go.com/nba/story/_/id /15172706/the-warriors-secret-sauce-team-dinners-road

Bronson, P., & Merryman, A. (2010, February 19). Just let them eat the marshmallow. *The Daily Beast.* Retrieved from http://www.thedailybeast.com /articles/2010/02/19/just-let-them-eat-the-marshmallow.html

Brooks, D. (2007, October 26). The outsourced brain. *New York Times.* Retrieved from http://www.nytimes.com/2007/10/26/opinion/26brooks.html

Brooks, D. (2011). *The social animal: The hidden sources of love, character, and achievement.* New York: Random House.

Brooks, D. (2015). *The road to character.* New York: Random House.

Brown, B. (2012). *Daring greatly: How the courage to be vulnerable transforms the way we live, love, parent, and lead.* New York: Spiegel & Grau.

Brown, B. (2013, December 10). *Brené Brown on empathy* [Video]. Available: https:// www.youtube.com/watch?v=1Evwgu369Jw

Brown, B. (2015). *Rising strong: The reckoning. The rumble. The revolution.* New York: Spiegel & Grau.

Bryant, A. (2015, July 11). Stewart Butterfield of Slack: Is empathy on your résumé? *New York Times.* Retrieved from http://www.nytimes.com/2015/07/12 /business/stewart-butterfield-of-slack-experience-with-empathy-required.html

Bryant, A. (2016, March 11). Grit goes further than genius. *New York Times.* Retrieved from http://www.nytimes.com/2016/03/13/business/anthony-foxx -grit-goes-further-than-genius.html

Cain, S. (2012). *Quiet: The power of introverts in a world that can't stop talking.* New York: Random House.

Carter, S. (1996). *Integrity.* New York: Basic Books.

Cassidy, J. (2012, September 5). The "new Obama": Michelle keeps hopes alive. *The New Yorker.* Retrieved from http://www.newyorker.com/news/john-cassidy /the-new-obama-michelle-keeps-hope-alive

Chapman, B. & Sosodia, R. (2015). *Everybody matters: The extraordinary power of caring for your people like family.* New York: Penguin Press.

Chua, A. (2011). *Battle hymn of the tiger mother.* New York: Penguin.

Cloud, H. (2006). *Integrity: The courage to meet the demands of reality.* New York: HarperBusiness.

Coates, T. (2015). *Between the world and me.* New York: Spiegel & Grau.

Coffman. C., & Sorensen, K. (2013). *Culture eats strategy for lunch.* Denver, CO: Liang Addison Press.

Coleman, J. (2013, May 6). Six components of a great corporate culture. *Harvard Business Review.* Retrieved from https://hbr.org/2013/05/six-components -of-culture

Collins, J. (2001). *Good to great: Why some companies make the leap . . . and others don't.* New York: HarperCollins.

Conserve Energy Future. (n.d.). Fifteen major current environmental problems. Retrieved from http://www.conserve-energy-future.com/15-current -environmental-problems.php

Cooper-Kahn, J., & Dietzel, L. (2008). *Late, lost, and unprepared: A parents' guide to helping children with executive functioning.* Bethesda, MD: Woodbine Press.

Costa, A. & Kallick, B. (2008). *Learning and leading with Habits of Mind.* Alexandria, VA: ASCD.

Crowley, B., & Saide, B. (2016, January 20). Building empathy in classrooms and schools. *Ed Week.* Retrieved from http://www.edweek.org/tm/articles /2016/01/20/building-empathy-in-classrooms-and-schools.html

Davidson, C. (2011). *Now you see it: How technology and brain science will transform schools and business for the 21st century.* New York: Penguin.

Davis, J. H. (2015, December 10). President Obama signs into law a rewrite of No Child Left Behind. *New York Times.* Retrieved from http://www.nytimes .com/2015/12/11/us/politics/president-obama-signs-into-law-a-rewrite -of-no-child-left-behind.html

Davis-Laack, P. (2014, October 23). Grit: Your secret success strategy. *Paula Davis Laack.* Retrieved from http://www.pauladavislaack.com/grit-your-secret -success-strategy

DePree, M. (1990). *Leadership is an art.* New York: Dell.

Dickens, C. (1859/1999). *A tale of two cities.* New York: Dover Publications.

Dictionary.com. (n.d.). Retrieved from http://www.dictionary.com/browse /embrace?s=t

Didion, J. (1980). Why I write. In J. Sternburg (Ed.), *The writer on her work* (pp. 17–25). New York: W. W. Norton.

Duckworth, A. (2013, April). *Grit: The power of passion and perseverance* [Video]. Available: http://www.ted.com/talks/angela_lee_duckworth_the_key_to _success_grit.html

Duckworth, A. (2016). *Grit: The power of passion and perseverance.* New York: Simon & Schuster.

Duckworth, A., Peterson, C. Matthews, M., & Kelly, D. (2007). Grit: Perseverance and passion for long-term goals. *Journal of Personal and Social Psychology, 92*(6), 1087–1101.

Duhigg, C. (2012). *The power of habit: Why we do what we do in life and business.* New York: Random House.

Duhigg, C. (2016). *Smarter, faster, better: The secrets of being productive in life and in business.* New York: Random House.

Duncan, A. (2015, December 3). Secretary Duncan: 'Finally a fix to No Child Left Behind.' *White House Government Blog.* Retrieved from https://www.whitehouse .gov/blog/2015/12/03/secretary-arne-duncan-finally-fix-to-no-child-left-behind

Edmonds, S. C. (2014). *The culture engine: A framework for driving results, inspiring your employees, and transforming your workplace.* Hoboken, NJ: John Wiley & Sons.

el Kaliouby, R. (2015, May). *This app can tell how you feel—from the look on your face* [Video]. Available: https://www.ted.com/talks/rana_el_kaliouby_this_app _knows_how_you_feel_from_the_look_on_your_face

Elliott, J. (2006). *Jane Elliott's Blue Eyes/Brown Eyes exercise.* Available: http://www .janeelliott.com

Ellis, J. (2015). *The quartet: Orchestrating the second American Revolution, 1783–1789.* New York: Knopf.

Every Student Succeeds Act of 2015. Public law 114-95.

Executive function skills and disorders. (2016). *WebMD.* Available: http://www.webmd.com/add-adhd/guide/executive-function

Firestone, L. (2016, March 16). Why we need to teach kids emotional intelligence. *Psychology Today.* Available: https://www.psychologytoday.com/blog/compassion-matters/201603/why-we-need-teach-kids-emotional-intelligence

Fleischman, P. (1997). *Seedfolks.* New York: HarperTrophy.

Folger, T. (2015, August 27). Oceans will rise much more than predicted, NASA says. *National Geographic.* retrived from http://news.nationalgeographic.com/2015/08/150827-NASA-climate-oceans-seas-greenland

Frey, T. (2014, March). Thirty-three dramatic predictions for 2030. *Journal of Environmental Health, 76*(7), 52–54.

Friedman, T. (2005). *The world is flat: A brief history of the twenty-first century.* New York: Farrar, Straus, and Giroux.

Friedman, T. (2012, August 8). Average is over, Part II. *New York Times.* Retrieved from http://www.nytimes.com/2012/08/08/opinion/friedman-average-is-over-part-ii-.html

Fullan, M. (2014). *The principal: Three keys to maximizing impact.* New York: John Wiley.

Gardner, H. (1983). *Frames of mind: The theory of multiple intelligences.* New York: Basic Books.

Gardner, H. (2006). *Five minds for the future.* Cambridge, MA: Harvard Business School Press.

Gladwell, M. (2008). *The outliers: The story of success.* New York: Little, Brown & Company.

Glover, J. (2012, September 17). Defining brand strength: Differentiation & relevance. *Santafe.com.* Available: http://santafe.com/blogs/read/defining-brand-strength-differentiation-relevance

Gold, J. (2016, January 11). Teaching about stereotypes 2.0. *Teaching Tolerance.* Retrieved from http://www.tolerance.org/blog/teaching-about-stereotypes-20

Goleman, D. (1995). *Emotional intelligence: Why it can matter more than IQ.* New York: Bantam Press.

Goleman, D. (2006). *Social intelligence: The new science of human relationships.* New York: Bantam Press.

Goodwin, D. (2005). *Team of rivals: The political genius of Abraham Lincoln.* New York: Simon & Schuster.

Graham, B. (2008). *How to heal a broken wing.* Somerville, MA: Candlewick Press.

Halverson, H. G. (2011, November 2011). The trouble with bright kids. *Harvard Business Review.* Retrieved from https://hbr.org/2011/11/the-trouble-with-bright-kids

Hambrick, D. (2015, May 26). How smart should a president be? *Scientific American.* Retrieved from http://www.scientificamerican.com/article/how-smart-should-the-president-be/

Hart, C. (2014). *High price: A neuroscientist's journey of self-discovery that challenges everything you know about drugs and society.* New York: HarperCollins.

Heckman, J. (2013). *Giving kids a fair chance.* Cambridge, MA: MIT Press.

Heick, T. (2015, February 10). Teaching empathy: Are we teaching content or students? *Edutopia.* Retrieved from http://www.edutopia.org/blog/teaching -empathy-content-or-students-terry-heick

Herold, B. (2015, January 24). Is grit racist? *Education Week.* Retrieved from http:// blogs.edweek.org/edweek/DigitalEducation/2015/01/is_grit_racist.html

Hess, F. (2013). *Cage-busting leadership.* Cambridge, MA: Harvard Education Press.

Hillenbrand, L. (2010). *Unbroken: A World War II story of survival, resilience, and redemption.* New York: Random House.

Hoerr, T. (2005). *The art of school leadership.* Alexandria, VA: ASCD.

Hoerr, T. (2008/2009, December/January). Data that count. *Educational Leadership, 66*(4), 93–94.

Hoerr, T. (2009, July 23). MI Theory: A tool for differentiation. *ASCD Express.* Available: http://www.ascd.org/ascd-express/vol4/421-toc.aspx

Hoerr, T. (2012, March). Got grit? *Educational Leadership, 69*(6), 84–85.

Hoerr, T. (2013a). *Fostering grit: How do I prepare my students for the real world?* Alexandria, VA: ASCD.

Hoerr, T. (2013b). Good failures. *Educational Leadership, 71*(1), 84–85.

Hoerr, T. (2014). What's your favorite interview question? *Educational Leadership, 71*(5), 84–85.

Hoerr, T. (2015, February 17). 'Grit' helps everyone gain real-world success. Retrieved from http://www.newcityschool.org/uploads/miscellaneous/Grit .EW.both.pdf

Hoerr, T. (2015). Responding to Ferguson. *Educational Leadership, 72*(6), 85–86.

Hoerr, T. (2016a). Good failures: Great successes. *Independent School, 75*(2), pp. 88–92.

Hoerr, T. (2016b). Why you need a diversity champion. *Educational Leadership, 73*(7), 86–87.

Holmes, A. (2015, October 27). Has diversity lost its meaning? *New York Times Magazine.* Retrieved from http://www.nytimes.com/2015/11/01/magazine /has-diversity-lost-its-meaning.html

Homans, G. (1958). Social behavior as exchange. *American Journal of Sociology, 63*(6), 597–606.

Hough, L. (2015, January 8). What's worth learning in school? *Harvard Ed.* Retrieved from https://www.gse.harvard.edu/news/ed/15/01/whats -worth-learning-school

Itzkoff, D. (2015, October 23). Andy Kaufman and Redd Foxx to tour, years after death, as holograms. *New York Times.* Retrieved from http://www.nytimes .com/2015/10/24/arts/andy-kaufman-and-redd-foxx-to-tour-years-after-death .html

Jaggi, M. (2010, June 11). A life in writing: Barbara Kingsolver. *The Guardian.* Retrieved from https://www.theguardian.com/books/2010/jun/12/life-in -writing-barbara-kingsolver

Jensen, K. (2012, April 12). Intelligence is overrated: What you really need to succeed. *Forbes*. Available: http://www.forbes.com/sites/keldjensen/2012/04/12/intelligence-is-overrated-what-you-really-need-to-succeed

Kahn, A., & Bouie, J. (2015, June 25). The Atlantic slave trade in two minutes. *Slate*. Retrieved from http://www.slate.com/articles/life/the_history_of_american_slavery/2015/06/animated_interactive_of_the_history_of_the_atlantic_slave_trade.html

Kaiser Family Foundation. (2010). Generation M^2: Media in the lives of 8- to 18-year-olds. Retrieved from https://kaiserfamilyfoundation.files.wordpress.com/2013/04/8010.pdf

Kaiser Family Foundation. (2015, November 24). New KFF/CNN survey on race finds deep divisions in how blacks, whites and Hispanics experience and view race relations, discrimination, and the police. Retrieved from http://kff.org/other/press-release/new-kffcnn-survey-on-race-finds-deep-divisions-in-how-blacks-whites-and-hispanics-experience-and-view-race-relations-discrimination-and-the-police/

Kaplan, R. (2012). *The revenge of geography: What the map tells us about coming conflicts and the battle against fate*. New York: Random House.

Karp, S. (2013, fall). Charter schools and the future of public education. *Rethinking Schools, 28*(1). Retrieved from http://www.rethinkingschools.org/archive/28_01/28_01_karp.shtml

Kaufman, C. (2010). *Executive function in the classroom*. Baltimore, MD: Paul H. Brookes Publishing.

Kay, K., & Greenhill, V. (2012). *The leader's guide to 21st-century skills: Seven steps for schools and districts*. Boston: Allyn & Bacon.

Kovacs, P. (2015, February 19). Is there school today? *Huffington Post*. Retrieved from http://www.huffingtonpost.com/philip-kovacs/is-there-school-today_b_6712590.html

Krznaric, R. (2014). *Empathy: Why it matters, and how to get it*. New York: Random House.

Kunstler, J. H. (2005). *The long emergency: Surviving the converging catastrophes of the 21st century*. New York: Grove Atlantic.

Kurzweil, R. (1999). *The age of spiritual machines: When computers exceed human intelligence*. New York: Viking.

Kurzweil, R. (2011, December 9). Singularity Q&A. *Kurzweil Accelerated Intelligence*. Available: http://www.kurzweilai.net/singularity-q-a

Kurzweil, R. (2015, December 9). How to animate a digital model of a person from images collected from the Internet. *Kurzweil Accelerated Intelligence*. Available: http://www.kurzweilai.net/how-to-animate-a-digital-model-of-a-person-from-images-collected-from-the-internet

Lafrance, Adrian. (2015, September 30) How many websites are there? *The Atlantic*. Retrieved from http://www.theatlantic.com/technology/archive/2015/09/how-many-websites-are-there/408151/

Lahey, J. (2013, January 29). Why parents need to let their children fail. *The Atlantic*. Retrieved from http://www.theatlantic.com/national/archive/2013/01/why-parents-need-to-let-their-children-fail/272603

Lahey, J. (2014, September 4). Teaching children empathy. *New York Times*. Retrieved from http://parenting.blogs.nytimes.com/2014/09/04/teaching-children-empathy/

Larson, E. (2011). *In the garden of beasts: Love, terror, and an American family in Hitler's Berlin*. New York: Broadway Paperbacks.

Lee, H. (1960). *To kill a mockingbird*. New York: Grand Central Publishing.

Leovy, J. (2015). *Ghettoside: A true story of murder in America*. New York: Spiegel & Grau.

Lewis, L. (2013, May 2). 26 shockingly bad predictions. *Buzzfeed*. Retrieved from www.buzzfeed.com/lukelewis/26-shockingly-bad-predictions

Lowry, L. (1993). *The giver*. New York: Houghton-Mifflin.

Ludwig, T. & Barton, P. (2013). *The invisible boy*. New York: Knopf.

Machine earning: Jobs in poor countries may be especially vulnerable to automation. (2016, January 30). *The Economist*. Retrieved from http://www.economist.com/news/finance-and-economics/21689635-jobs-poor-countries-may-be-especially-vulnerable-automation-machine-earning

Mankins, M. C. (2013, December). The defining elements of a winning culture. *Harvard Business Review*. Retrieved from https://hbr.org/2013/12/the-definitive-elements-of-a-winning-culture

Maslow, A. (1943). A theory of human motivation. *Psychological Review, 50*(4), 370–396.

McChrystal, S. (2015). *Team of teams: New rules of engagement for a complex world*. New York: Penguin.

McCloud, C. & Messing, D. (2006). *Have you filled a bucket today: A guide to daily happiness for kids*. Northville, MI: Ferne Press.

McGovern, M. (Ed.). (2016). *The 2015–2016 NAIS Trendbook*. Washington, DC: NAIS Press.

Menzel, M., & Mann, C. (1995). *Material world: A global family portrait*. Berkeley, CA: Ten Speed Press.

Menzel, M., & Mann, C. (2005). *Hungry planet: What the world eats*. Berkeley, CA: Ten Speed Press.

Merriam Webster. (n.d.). Retrieved from http://www.merriam-webster.com/dictionary/integrity

Meyer, D. (2008). *Setting the table: The transforming power of hospitality in business*. New York: Harper Perennial.

Miles, K. (2015, October 1). Ray Kurzweil: In the 2030s, nanobots in our brains will make us "godlike." *The Huffington Post*. Retrieved from http://www.huffingtonpost.com/entry/ray-kurzweil-nanobots-brain-godlike_us_560555a0e4b0af3706dbe1e2

Milgram, S. (1963). Behavioral study of obedience. *Journal of Abnormal and Social Psychology, 67*(4), 371–378.

Miller, A. (1953). *The Crucible*. New York: Penguin Press.

Miller, C. C. (2014, December 15). As robots grow smarter, American workers struggle to keep up. *New York Times*. Retrieved from http://www.nytimes.com/2014/12/16/upshot/as-robots-grow-smarter-american-workers-struggle-to-keep-up.html

Mischel, W. (2014). *The Marshmallow Test: Mastering self-control.* New York: Little, Brown & Company.

Murphy, K. (2013, April 20). Maya Angelou. *New York Times* Retrieved from http://www.nytimes.com/2013/04/21/opinion/sunday/a-chat-with-maya-angelou.html?_r=0

National Commission on Excellence in Education. (1983). *A nation at risk: The imperative for educational reform.* Washington, DC: Author.

NBC Nightly News with Lester Holt. (2015, November 2). Study: Nearly 8 in 10 toddlers use mobile devices daily. *NBC Nightly News with Lester Holt.* Available: http://www.nbcnews.com/nightly-news/video/study—nearly-8-in-10-toddlers-use-mobile-device-daily-557608003605

Nike. (2005, December 13). *Michael Jordan: Failure* [Video]. Available: http://www.youtube.com/watch?v=8HkGmRShkjI

NPR staff. (2015, April 5). The power and problem of grit. *Hidden Brain* [Radio series]. Retrieved from http://www.npr.org/2016/04/04/472162167/the-power-and-problem-of-grit

Obama, B. (2006, June 19). Obama to graduates: Cultivate empathy. Retrieved from http://www.northwestern.edu/newscenter/stories/2006/06/barack.html

Palacio, R. (2012). *Wonder.* New York: Random House.

Patel, E. (2015, October 15). Presentation to the ISACS Board of Directors, Chicago, IL.

Preston, J. (2015, September 28). Share of immigrants in U.S. nears high of early 20th century, report finds. *New York Times.* Retrieved from http://www.nytimes.com/2015/09/28/us/share-of-immigrants-in-us-nears-highs-of-early-20th-century-report-finds.html

Randall, E. (2012, November 9). Mitt Romney was ready to troll Boston with fireworks if he won. *Boston.* Retrieved from http://www.bostonmagazine.com/news/blog/2012/11/09/mitt-romney-ready-troll-boston-fireworks-won/

Razza, R., Bergen-Cico, D., & Raymond, K. (2015). Enhancing preschoolers' self-regulation via mindful yoga. *Journal of Child and Family Studies, 24*(2), 372–385. Retrieved from https://www.researchgate.net/publication/258163321_Enhancing_Preschoolers%27_Self-Regulation_Via_Mindful_Yoga

Rennie Center, & ASCD. (2016). *Social and emotional learning: Opportunities for Massachusetts, lessons for the nation.* Washington, DC: Authors.

Ross, C. (2016). *The industries of the future.* New York: Simon & Schuster.

Rotman, D. (2013, June 12). How technology is destroying jobs. *MIT Technology Review.* Retrieved from https://www.technologyreview.com/s/515926/how-technology-is-destroying-jobs/

Schultz, H. (2010, October 9). Good C.E.O.'s are insecure (and know it). *New York Times.* Retrieved from http://www.nytimes.com/2010/10/10/business/10corner.html

Schwartz, A. (2013, February 26). In Cisco's classroom of the future, your professor is just an illusion. *Fast Company.* Retrieved from http://www.fastcoexist.com/1681458/in-ciscos-classroom-of-the-future-your-professor-is-just-an-illusion

Segran, E. (2015, June 24). What emotion-reading computers are learning about us. *Fast Company.* Retrieved from http://www.fastcompany.com/3047431/most-creative-people/what-emotion-reading-computers-are-learning-about-us

SelfControl. (n.d.). Available: http://www.selfcontrolapp.com.

Sinek, S. (2011). *Start with why: How great leaders inspire everyone to take action.* New York: Penguin.

Singal, J. (2016, January 6). Want to end bullying? Get the popular students to help. *New York Times Magazine.* Retrieved from http://nymag.com/scienceofus /2016/01/end-bullying-get-the-cool-kids-to-help.html

Singleton, G. E. (2015). *Courageous conversations about race: A field guide for achieving equity in schools* (2nd ed.). Thousand Oaks, CA: Corwin.

Smith, C., McGovern, G., Larson, R., Hillaker, B., & Peck, S. C. (2016). *Preparing youth to thrive: Promising practices in social and emotional learning.* Washington, DC: Forum for Youth Investment.

Southern Poverty Law Center. (2016). Examining your school's climate. Available: http://www.tolerance.org/map-it-out

Statistic Brain. Gym membership statistics. Available: http://www.statisticbrain .com/gym-membership-statistics

Steele, C. (1999, August). Thin ice: Black stereotypes and college students. *The Atlantic.* Retrieved from http://www.theatlantic.com/magazine/archive /1999/08/thin-ice-stereotype-threat-and-black-college-students/304663

Steele, C. (2010). *Whistling Vivaldi and other clues to how stereotypes affect us.* New York: W.W. Norton & Company.

Steinbeck, J. (1939). *The grapes of wrath.* New York: Penguin.

Street, F. (2011, May 15). What IQ tests really measure. *Business Insider.* Retrieved from www.businessinsider.com/what-iq-tests-really-measure-2011-5

Sullivan, A. (2015, December 2). The limitations of teaching grit in the classroom. *The Atlantic.* Retrieved from http://www.theatlantic.com/education /archive/2015/12/when-grit-isnt-enough/418269

Surowiecki, J. (2004). *The wisdom of crowds: Why the many are smarter than the few and how collective wisdom shapes business, economies, societies, and nations.* New York: Anchor.

Swarns, R. L. (2016, April 17). 272 slaves were sold to Georgetown University. What does it owe their descendants? *New York Times.* Retrieved from http:// www.nytimes.com/2016/04/17/us/georgetown-university-search-for-slave -descendants.html

Swarns, R. L. (2016, June 14). Moving to make amends, Georgetown president meets with descendant of slaves. *New York Times.* Retrieved from http://www .nytimes.com/2016/06/15/us/moving-to-make-amends-georgetown-president -meets-with-descendant-of-slaves.html?ref=todayspaper&_r=0

Tavangar, H. (2014, August 7). Empathy: The most important back-to-school sup- ply. *Edutopia.* Available: http://www.edutopia.org/blog/empathy-back-to -school-supply-homa-tavangar

Theroux, P. (2015). *Deep south: Four seasons on back roads.* New York: Houghton-Mifflin.

Thomas, J. (2011, August 15). Honesty is not synonymous with integrity, and we need to know the difference, for integrity is what we need. *Alliance for Integrity*

website. Available: http://allianceforintegrity.com/integrity-articles/honesty-is
-not-synonymous-with-integrityand-we-need-to-know-the-differencefor
-integrity-is-what-we-need/

Thomson, B. J. (1993). *Words can hurt you: Beginning a program of anti-bias education.*
Menlo Park, CA: Addison-Wesley.

Tough, P. (2009, September 27). Can the right kind of play teach self-control?
New York Times. Retrieved from http://www.nytimes.com/2009/09/27
/magazine/27tools-t.html

Tough, P. (2011, November 18). What if the secret to success is failure? *New York
Times Magazine*. Retrieved from http://www.nytimes.com/2011/09/18
/magazine/what-if-the-secret-to-success-is-failure.html

Tough, P. (2012). *How children succeed: Grit, curiosity, and the hidden power of character.* New York: Random House.

Tough, P. (2016). *Helping children succeed: What works and why.* New York: Hough-
ton Mifflin Harcourt.

Turkle, S. (2015). *Reclaiming conversation: The power of talk in a digital age.* New York:
Penguin.

Vanek, C. (2015, December 17). Empathy reigns. *Arizona Daily Sun*. Retrieved from
http://azdailysun.com/news/local/empathy-reigns/article_5c915130-232
e-5c5b-ac05-aca852329c31.html

Wayne, T. (2015, October 11). Found on Facebook: Empathy. *New York Times*.
Retrieved from http://www.nytimes.com/2015/10/11/fashion/found-on
-facebook-empathy.html

Weir, R. (2012, January). The power of self-control. *APA Monitor*, 43(1), 36.

Wheeler, S. (2014, April 28). Can mindfulness help kids learn self-control? *Greater
Good*. Retrieved from http://www.greatergood.berkeley.edu/article/item
/mindfulness_help_kids_learn_self_control

Wright, J. (2009). The general theory: Self-control. *Oxford Bibliographies*.
Retrieved from http://www.oxfordbibliographies.com/view/document
/obo-9780195396607/obo-9780195396607-0004.xml

Zernike, K. (2016, February 29). Testing for joy and grit? Schools nationwide push
to measure students' emotional skills. *New York Times*. Retrieved from http://
www.nytimes.com/2016/03/01/us/testing-for-joy-and-grit-schools-nationwide
-push-to-measure-students-emotional-skills.html

Zimbardo, P. G. (2016). The Stanford Prison Experiment: A simulation on the psychology of imprisonment. Retrieved from http://www.prisonexp.org

Index

The use of *f* following a page number denotes a figure.

About the Author

Thomas R. Hoerr retired after leading the New City School in St. Louis, Missouri, for 34 years and is now the Emeritus Head of School. He teaches at the University of Missouri–St. Louis and holds a PhD from Washington University in St. Louis. Hoerr has written four books—*Becoming a Multiple Intelligences School* (2000), *The Art of School Leadership* (2005), *School Leadership for the Future* (2009), and *Fostering Grit* (2013)—and more than 100 articles, including "The Principal Connection" column in *Educational Leadership*. Hoerr is an enthusiastic but poor basketball player. Readers who would like to continue the dialogue may contact him at trhoerr@newcityschool.org or trhoerr@aol.com.

Acknowledgments

I have been talking about the personal intelligences since the 1980s and writing about success for more than a decade, but bringing it all together in a book was a new and difficult experience. I could not have done it without the help of many friends and colleagues. Naming the people who helped me on this book—those who offered specific information and suggestions and those who provided the context for it to be written—is both fun and a bit daunting. I love the thought of publicly thanking and recognizing these people; that's fun! But listing their names is also daunting because I worry that someone will be omitted. As has been the case throughout my career, I am indebted to so many people for whatever successes I have achieved.

First, a big hug of appreciation goes to the faculty of the New City School and everyone in our school community. For 34 years I was fortunate to work—to live—in a setting in which student growth was the focus and children were viewed through all of their intelligences. I was surrounded by and learned from remarkably talented teachers and administrators. Within that group, special gratitude goes to Joe Corbett, Carla Duncan, Laurie Falk, Ben Griffiths, Eileen Griffiths, Nina Nichols, Stephanie Teachout, and Chris Wallach for their input on this book. Thanks, too, to the New City School Board of Trustees for recognizing that there are differences between success in life and success in school, and for supporting my growth. Not a day passed that I didn't think *I wish that I had attended New City School.*

Historically (and I am old enough to begin a paragraph like that), thanks go to the teachers and professors who pushed and supported me when I was officially a student. That begins with my 1st grade teacher at Monroe School, Mrs. Helen Mayfield, and also includes professors Barry Anderson, Dave Colton, Charles Fazzaro, and, especially, Roger Perry. Howard Gardner deserves special thanks for his ongoing support, confidence, and friendship. Thanks also to the students in my spring 2016 Ed. Admin. 6705 class at the University of Missouri–St. Louis. I learned from them.

Many, many people took the time to offer suggestions, share ideas, or critique my thinking. This book is better because of them and any errors are owned by me. Thank you, Carly Andrews, Nick Apperson, Kristi Arbetter, Bonnie Barczykowski, Carole Basile, Michelle Benginga, Jeffrey Benson, Marvin Berkowitz, Robert Brisk, Lisa Brougham, Jennifer Bryan, Pat Brubaker, Mark Catalana, Naoimh Campbell, Sheryl Chard, Rob Ciampoli, Tom Cody, Alan Cooper, Clark Daggett, Claudia Daggett, Tom Davey, Matthew Davis, John Delautre, Chris Dornfeld, Kevin Dwyer, Diane Dymond, Vince Estrada, Paul Fanuele, Ginny Fendell, Patrick Fisher, Mike Fleetham, Sharon Friesen, Laura Fuller, Andrew Gallager, Matthew Gould, Karen Guskin, Billy Handmaker, Maureen Hanlon, Sharonica Hardin, Gastrid Harrigan, Mark Harrington, Terry Harris, Chris Hass, Joanna Hastings, Jason Heiserer, Craig Hinkle, Deb Holmes, Dawn Isaacs, Jarin Jaffee, Charles James, Misty Johnson, Gina Kietzmann, Brian King, DuWayne Krause, Stephanie Krauss, Jeff Lowell, Kim Marshall, Peter Martin, Ellen Matthews, Rick Mesich, Kathy Mueller, Mark Norwood, George Peternel, Melanie Pruitt, Cheryl Roberts, Gema Zamarro Rodriguez, Jenny Rowe, John Sandberg, Caryn Sawlis, Jessie Schoolman, Dan Schwartz, Nell Sears, Keith Shahan, Carrie Steinbach, Barbara Thomson, Elizabeth Towner, Alden Weaver, Amy Yount, and Larry Zarin.

In an effort to obtain some balance in my life, I want to give a shout-out to my semi-monthly book group and my Saturday morning basketball buddies. I should also note that I appreciate their reluctance to call my fouls.

Applause also goes to the ASCD staff who took this dream to reality, beginning with Genny Ostertag, director of Content Acquisitions. She offered enthusiasm, wisdom, and great ideas. This book would not have happened without the support of Liz Wegner and fine editing skills of Ernesto Yermoli. Thanks to *Educational Leadership* editor-in-chief Marge Scherer for her confidence throughout the years with "The Principal Connection" column. Writing the column has been very helpful to me, because as Peter Elbow said, "Writing is a way to end up thinking something you couldn't have started out thinking."

A sense of deep gratitude goes to my aunt and uncle, Mary Lou Keller and Jim Wurm, for their ongoing care and to my mom and dad for their love and genes. And this book could not have been written without the support of my wife, Karleen, and companionship of our dog, Onyx (who really doesn't think he's a dog).

Finally, thanks to all of the hardworking and caring educators who seek to change their students' lives. I hope that this book can be a useful tool.

Related ASCD Resources

At the time of publication, the following ASCD resources were available (ASCD stock numbers in parentheses). For up-to-date information about ASCD resources, go to www.ascd.org. Search the complete archives of *Educational Leadership* at www.ascd.org/el.

ASCD Edge®

Exchange ideas and connect with other educators interested in social and emotional learning on the social networking site ASCD Edge® at http://edge.ascd.org.

Print Products

Fostering Grit: How do I prepare my students for the real world? (ASCD Arias) by Thomas R. Hoerr (#SF113075)

The Art of School Leadership by Thomas R. Hoerr (#105037)

Fostering Resilient Learners: Strategies for Creating a Trauma-Sensitive Classroom by Kristin Souers with Pete Hall (#116014)

The Power of the Adolescent Brain: Strategies for Teaching Middle and High School Students by Thomas Armstrong (#116017)

Encouragement in the Classroom: How do I help students stay positive and focused? (ASCD Arias) by Joan Young (#SF114049)

Educational Leadership: Learning for Life (March 2016) (#116033)

Educational Leadership: Emotionally Healthy Kids (October 2015) (#116029)

PD Online® Courses

Embracing Diversity: Managing Diverse Schools and Classrooms, 2nd Edition (#PD11OC124M)

Embracing Diversity: Effective Teaching, 2nd Edition (#PD11OC123M)

For more information: send e-mail to member@ascd.org; call 1-800-933-2723 or 703-578-9600, press 2; send a fax to 703-575-5400; or write to Information Services, ASCD, 1703 N. Beauregard St., Alexandria, VA 22311-1714 USA.